DATE DUE

Contemporary Studies
of Swift's Poetry

Contemporary Studies of Swift's Poetry

Editors
John Irwin Fischer
Donald C. Mell, Jr.

Associate Editor
David M. Vieth

Newark
University of Delaware Press
London and Toronto Associated University Presses

© 1981 by Associated University Presses, Inc.

Associated University Presses, Inc.
4 Cornwall Drive
East Brunswick, New Jersey 08816

Associated University Presses
69 Fleet Street
London EC4Y 1EU, England

Associated University Presses
Toronto M5E 1A7, Canada

Library of Congress Cataloging in Publication Data
Main entry under title:

Contemporary studies of Swift's poetry.

Includes index.
   1. Swift, Jonathan, 1667–1745—Poetic works—
Addresses, essays, lectures.   I. Fischer, John Irwin,
1940–   II. Mell, Donald Charles.   III. Vieth,
David M.
PR3728.P58C6   821'.5   79-21610
ISBN 0-87413-173-1

Printed in the United States of America

IN MEMORIAM
Maurice Johnson

Contents

Acknowledgments

For permission to include materials published in other forms elsewhere, the editors thank *Papers on Language and Literature*, Bucknell University Press (*Energy and Order in the Poetry of Swift*, A. B. England); The University of Wisconsin Press (*The Poetry of Jonathan Swift: Allusion and the Development of a Poetic Style*, Peter J. Schakel); The University Press of Kentucky (*The Impossible Observer: Reason and the Reader in 18th-Century Prose*, Robert W. Uphaus).

We are also grateful to the University of Delaware, Louisiana State University, and Southern Illinois University at Carbondale for a variety of grants, favors, and library kindnesses. Without the enthusiastic support of numerous friends, colleagues, and associates this volume would not have been possible. We wish to thank especially Jerry Beasley, Leo Lemay, Elaine Safer, Jack Gilbert, and Herbert Rothschild for their thoughtful suggestions and support. Both Cathryn McCarthy and Derek van Bever worked hard and long securing and assembling library materials and checking notes and references. Deborah Lyall and the secretarial staff of the University of Delaware English Department deserve a note of thanks for the long hours spent helping to prepare the manuscript. Derek van Bever compiled the index.

We thank James Merrill and the Board of Editors of the University of Delaware Press for their continued encouragement and help during the editing process. Barbara Tieger expertly guided the volume through press, and we are grateful for her sound editorial advice.

Finally, we thank Panthea Reid Broughton, Katherine L. Mell, and Rose S. Vieth for shrewd advice, generous comment, and patience.

Introduction: "All . . . Manifestly Deduceable"

In the fall of 1975, several of us who had found Swift's poetry increasingly attractive began to wonder how many of our colleagues shared our experience. On the evidence of recent publication, it appeared that interest in Swift's verse was higher than at any time since the poet's death, but none of us knew how extensive, deep, or shapely that interest might be. In order to find out, David M. Vieth took responsibility for chairing a Special Session on Swift's poetry at the 1976 annual meeting of the Modern Language Association. The response to that Session was overwhelming, generating such a rich mixture of topics and viewpoints as to make subsequent Sessions appropriate at both the 1977 and 1978 MLA meetings. As a result of those meetings, it now seems right to take stock of where we have been, to consider what we have learned, and to make some predictions.

These goals are ambitious ones to aim at in the first collection of essays devoted exclusively to Swift's poetry, but the essays collected in this volume have special histories. Nearly all of them have been presented in both oral and written form to the one hundred or so Swiftians gathered for each Special Session. Consequently, many have been modified since their presentation to reflect the diverse opinions, suggestions, and objections they encountered. In addition, the authors of these essays have published numerous articles and books on Swift's poetry. Because these essays are, then, the responses of experienced scholars to specific chal lenges in and arising from Swift's poetry, they represent, as fully as is possible within a single volume, our current understanding of Swift's canon and its relationship to the forms of Augustan poetry.

For some time now, that understanding has been developing. In the past, conditioned by our study of other poets, many of us argued as if Swift's verse must either reflect or reject the dominant literary culture in which it was written. Significantly, we made no such demand of Swift's prose. But in verse we wished Swift to speak as either a closet Augustan or as a consistent eccentric. Because he is neither, in prose or in verse, our expectations distorted our efforts; too often we failed to read Swift's poems in light of the specific ends and principles of construction that governed their composition.

Most previous essays on Swift's verse can be classified under one of three critical approaches or some combination of them. The first approach is biobibliographical. Because Swift was notoriously careless about preserving most of his poetry, not until Sir Harold Williams's 1937 edition of the poems (revised 1958) could a serious reader of the verse readily afford to trust the authority of the text he was using. Worse, the canonical authenticity of many poems was questionable. Understandably, then, for many of this century's best Swiftians, to write of Swift's verse was to write bibliographically. Further, since most bibliographical questions require answers that are partly biographical, to write of Swift's verse was also to involve oneself deeply in the events of Swift's life. Under such circumstances, for many critics biographical occasion merged with poetic significance, and the problems posed by Swift's literary methods were submerged. Despite this limitation, biobibliographical inquiry into Swift's verse served us well, resulting in the establishment of a sturdy, though not, as

Aubrey L. Williams's bibliographically prescient essay suggests and as James Woolley's model sequel to that essay demonstrates, an unquestionable canon.

The consequences of a second approach to Swift's verse are, in Mark Twain's fine phrase, more various. This approach developed out of, and depends upon, two assumptions: first, that it is the usual business of poetry to transcend the everyday world and to turn its contents into something new and strange; second, that Swift made it his business as a poet to take the contents of poetry and, by demythologizing those contents, to return them to the reality from whence they sprang. The proponents of this approach developed so holistic a view of Swift's achievement in verse that they dubbed nearly all his poetry "anti-poetry" and called Swift himself an "anti-poet."

The "anti-poetry" approach to Swift's verse produced some notable ironies. In their zeal to reduce Swift to a realist's realist, readers working within this approach alerted us to the frequency with which Swift took over and turned to his own purposes everything from whole poetic genres to individual lines borrowed from obscure poems and alluded to by, perhaps, single words. Thus, seeking to demonstrate how much of his literary inheritance Swift distrusted and disowned, such readers brought a world of richness to his verse. Because of their biases, however, they remained unimpressed by what they found. Like men who maintain the illogical and impoverishing view that the only truth is that there is no truth, they maintained that Swift's only icon was iconoclasm.

The third traditional approach to Swift's poetry, a rhetorical approach, provided needed correctives to the approaches already outlined but produced imbalances of its own. The central assumption of this more recent approach is that the value of Swift's poetry primarily consists neither in the originality of its insights nor in the power of its message but rather in its fascinating adjustment of strategic means to intended ends. For the practitioners of this approach, Swift's poetic canon chiefly consists of a series of attempts to respond to two problems: first, that satire is a mirror in which people always tend to see everyone's face but their own; second, that while Swift's professed purpose in writing was usually moral, his motives for writing were often unsocial. According to this approach, then, to the extent that Swift solved these problems in individual poems, his poems are to be valued, but to the degree that Swift failed either to present himself attractively or to remonstrate with us tellingly, to that degree his poems fail.

Probably the greatest virtue of this approach is that it militates against a too-easy assumption either that the Swift we meet in any poem or any line is the historical Swift or that the apparent attacks Swift mounts on his poetic inheritance are to be understood as an ultimate rejection of that inheritance. Further, this approach encourages us to value at least some of the verbal playfulness that is one aspect of that wit Swift himself took as a defining mark of his quality as a writer. Nevertheless, a possible final effect of this approach is to make of Swift's canon a body of verse without a soul. For, viewed only as contrivance, the verse never appears to rise to the status of event: that is, the successful mingling of words with judgment, contrivance with circumstance, rhetorical skill with moral conviction that has no better definition than the act of a good man writing. Bluntly put, when untempered by a controlled concern for Swift, his audience, and the contexts of his verse, the rhetorical approach to Swift's poetry eviscerates his poems.

Not that the authors of this volume have rejected either the rhetorical approach or the other approaches described above. But these essays demonstrate a critical flexibility uncommon until recent years in Swift studies. For example, in "Fictive Self-Portraiture in Swift's Poetry," Louise K. Barnett raises a familiar question: what are we to make of the repetitively autobiographical character of much of Swift's canon? To answer this question Barnett necessarily turns over some old evidence; she examines, for instance, the disparities between the account Swift provides of himself in "Verses on the Death of Dr. Swift" and the account any one of us might give of him. Her interest in examining this evidence is not biographical, though, and neither is it thematic or rhetorical. For Barnett does not argue in behalf of a particular reading of individual poems, nor does she postulate a Swift carefully contemplating his technique in relation to his intentions. Rather, with numerous examples to illustrate her point, she argues that "in Swift's poetry, self tends to be its own end rather than a strategy for presenting something else." And if this argument produces one familiar conclusion, that in his verse Swift attempted to create a monument to self in order to guard his memory against "careless and ignorant posterity," it also yields two more provocative insights. First, Barnett argues, "behind the profusion of perspectives on self in Swift's poetry lies a modern sense of the mosaic of human personality, motivation, and perception—the complexity and ineluctability of self." Second, as Barnett puts it at the close of her argument, Swift's end as a verse writer was to *become* "the monument he himself constructed for posterity—the poetic memorial to self." If Barnett is right in these points, then Swift's verse is a very significant part of that debate over the nature of human personality that took place around and in the wake of Locke's psychological theories.

Another essay that works familiar questions into new insights is Robert W. Uphaus's "Swift's Irony Reconsidered." Uphaus begins by reminding us that, for F. R. Leavis, Swift's greatness as a writer sprang neither from "moral grandeur" nor from "human centrality" but simply from the negative intensity with which he wrote. Although Uphaus finds this argument more convincing as it applies to Swift's prose than others of us do, he sharply denies Leavis's further claim that the same argument can be extended to Swift's verse. Thus Uphaus maintains, as do several other essayists represented here, that, though equally startling in their methods, Swift's poetry and Swift's prose are markedly different literary phenomena. Uphaus explores their difference by observing that, in verse, Swift's force is not simply a matter of "presentment," which is to say, "the energy of Swift's presence," but also a function of Swift's actual "estimate of things . . . his personal convictions." In his late poems particularly, Uphaus argues, Swift's standard rhetorical complexities drop away, and, "no longer much interested in irony and satire . . . he is preoccupied with flat out attack and defense." Of course, as Uphaus recognizes, this argument nearly resurrects the artless Swift of biographical criticism, misanthropically flailing away at life itself. But the effect of Uphaus's essay, far from raising that old ghost, is instead to force us to find language to describe the interaction of plain speech and literary awareness that is the stuff of Swift's last great poems. *Contra* Leavis, Uphaus argues, the late poetry is not a place where literary criticism ought to stop, but "where any estimate of Swift's career might well begin."

Perhaps the most traditional essay in this collection, and the one most interesting to contrast with that of Uphaus, is A. B. England's "Rhetorical Order and Emotional Turbulence in 'Cadenus and Vanessa.' " In this essay England refines and expands on an impressive argument Gareth Jones made several years ago: that the protracted and fruitless debate between the characters in "Cadenus and Vanessa" finally exhibits the inadequacy of "naked reason" to tame "the chaotic world of sense and experience." By examining in careful detail the ways Swift punctures the elegant speeches of his characters and the elaborate framework of his own poem, England both reinforces Jones's original observations and demonstrates the power of a rhetorical approach to Swift's verse. But exactly because he uses his approach so scrupulously, England also establishes the limit of the rhetorical approach as a means to answer our legitimate questions about

Swift's verse. Confined to the treatment of text as patterned artifact, the method cannot admit either of instances of real authorial confusion or of moments of rhetorically unpatterned insight. Thus, in "Cadenus and Vanessa" the approach can show us how Swift undermined what Leavis called "the shallow commonplaces of Augustan Common Sense," but it cannot show us where, if anyplace, we stand in the presence of what Uphaus calls Swift's actual "estimate of things . . . his personal convictions." Implicit in England's excellent analysis is the truth that *if* there are any "positives" within the challenging environment of Swift's patterned ironies, we shall have to find them in other ways.

Two ways we might well explore are opened for us by Arthur H. Scouten in "Swift's Poetry and the Gentle Reader" and James Woolley in "Swift's 'Verses on the Death of Dr. Swift' as Autobiography." Both essayists are concerned with Swift's contexts. As befits the contribution of the senior Swiftian of this volume, Scouten's essay is partly admonitory. He reminds us that, though Swift almost always wrote for the "gentle reader," he sharply distinguished between poems written for the public and poems written for private persons. With poems of the latter sort, Scouten warns, we must avoid the temptation to "explicate" lines and passages written in private code, the "in-joke" language really intelligible only to the poem's recipients. More broadly, we must also recognize that many of even Swift's most "public" poems developed out of private contexts or we may mistake the nature of the universals they affirm, reading as dispassionate statements poems that are, as Scouten reminds us, "revised, polished, and expanded" versions of Swift's intimate view of himself and his world.

James Woolley warns us of this danger, too, and gives his warning special force by the method through which he illustrates it. Taking as his text the most hotly debated lines in Swift's poetic canon, the famous panegyric at the Rose, which completes "Verses on the Death of Dr. Swift," Woolley compares the facts, opinions, and sentiments expressed in that panegyric with similar expressions appearing in Swift's prose, primarily the correspondence. Of course, as Woolley notes, such comparison can never establish the *veracity* of the panegyric, but such comparison can demonstrate that the vision of Swift presented in the panegyric is, for the most part, Swift's real vision of himself. Simply knowing that this is so rescues us from many a possible false reading of the panegyric; analogously, the same method applied to other poems of Swift's must impose salutary restrictions on our responses to them. At its best, Woolley's method forces us to appreciate that the contexts that shaped Swift's values are sometimes idiosyncratic and almost always different from our own, a truth that should provoke us to continue Woolley's tentative explorations of those contexts.

Of course, to seek for contexts that may shape the turns of a Swift poem into single, sinuous sense is a delicate undertaking. Without care, a critic so engaged can easily become either a collector of trivial allusions or, worse, a Procrustes of poetry. What is wanted for such a search is that quality of acumen-tempered-by-reserve exhibited, though in strikingly different ways, in the essays of Richard H. Rodino, David M. Vieth, and Nora Crow Jaffe. Of these essays, Rodino's "Notes on the Developing Motives and Structures of Swift's Poetry" is plainly the boldest, in terms of both the background it postulates and the sweep of poems it encompasses. Rodino argues that if we view Swift's poetic canon against the prevailing eighteenth-century "belief that certain verse structures [have] power to deal with the conflicting demands of idealism and honesty," then that canon divides into four phases. In the first phase, the period of the early odes, Swift struggles to create conciliatory, omnivalent structures but is unable to do so. In the second phase (1698-1714), Swift succeeds in constructing a body of verse that appears to reconcile idealistic hope with matters of fact. In the third phase (1714-30), Swift's verse drifts toward an anarchic vision of a reality only serially organized or comprised of nebulous and competing perspectives. In the final and, Rodino argues, greatest phase, Swift reverses the poetic conventions he struggled to master in his youth and uses those conventions to "deceive the reader into affirming a normative position, a way of understanding the world in moral terms, that is then swept out from under him." As Rodino recognizes, his overview of Swift's poetic achievement is likely to spark controversy, both in its discussion of particular poems and in its discussion of backgrounds. Despite such potential controversy, his essay reminds us of our responsibility to describe the shape of Swift's canon in terms large enough to matter to the non-Swiftian and non-eighteenth-century specialist.

David M. Vieth's essay, "Metaphors and Metamorphoses: Poetic Techniques in the Middle Period of Swift's Career," forms an interesting complement to Rodino's work. Like Rodino, though with a slight disagreement about dates, Vieth argues that the years 1698 through 1719 mark a distinct period within Swift's canon. For Vieth, this period can be defined either through its figures (during it, Swift's verse is dominated by "transforming metaphors or metaphorical metamorphoses") or by its contexts ("It is by now a commonplace that many of Swift's poems, written between 1698 and 1719 . . . depict mock-Ovidian metamorphoses or mock-Christian miracles"). As every reader will notice, either definition opens the way for Vieth to develop insights about individual poems that tally very closely with Rodino's more theoretical conclusions. For example, both critics agree on the force of the broken metaphors Swift freely uses during this period. Vieth puts it one way (p. 61ff.), Rodino another (p. 91), but the agreement is startling. More startling still is the agreement, central to both essays, that during this period Swift did find a way, in Vieth's words, "to transform the raw stuff of life into high art." Yet, for all the agreement between these two critics about the shape and content of this period in Swift's canon, their essays are finally very different. To Rodino, the poems of this period are anomalous in Swift's canon and Swift himself an anomaly in the eighteenth century. To Vieth, the poems of this period are characteristic of Swift, and, viewed through them, Swift himself a recognizably eighteenth-century author.

In the face of such disagreement among experts, it is difficult not to throw up one's hands and say with the timid chorus in *Antigone,* "Both speak well." And, in a way that Nora Crow Jaffe's essay helps illuminate, such a response is probably the wisest one. In her essay, "Swift and the 'agreeable young Lady, but extremely lean,' " Jaffe never permits us to forget that "Death and Daphne" is, after all, an occasional piece, written quickly, and intended as entertainment for Sir Arthur and Lady Acheson. At the same time, by demonstrating for us the way Swift weaves into his poem not only the myths of Pluto and Proserpina and of Apollo and Daphne, but also his own relationship with Lady Acheson, Jaffe encourages us to find in the poem's meld of contexts a more complex statement of Swift's views on sex and poetry than Sir Arthur, his Lady, or even Swift himself probably recognized was there. Transcending the limits of the exegetical exercise she set herself, Jaffe implicitly demonstrates that at least some of Swift's poems are too vigorously alive for any element of the poem ever to exclude the presence of other elements. That is also, perhaps, the lesson to be drawn from the odd clash of agreements in the essays of Rodino and Vieth.

Indeed, it can be argued that every essay in this collection teaches this same lesson. For whether we are watching Peter J. Schakel reading the scatological poems by the light cast from Ovid's *Remedia Amoris,* or John Irwin Fischer examining the poems to Stella as types of Christian consolation, or Donald C. Mell placing the canon of Swift's verse alongside the tradition of mimetic literature, or James Woolley, in his generous second contribution to this volume, explaining the intricacies of early eighteenth-century editing and printing practices, we are repeatedly made conscious of two facts. The first is that Swift's verse draws on a much larger supply of literary and historical contexts than any one of us has yet fully mastered. Donna G. Fricke, in her study of Swift's background of English colloquial satire, David Sheehan, in his interpretation of Swift's early odes as satiric pindarics, and Aubrey L. Williams, in his reinterpretation of Swift's sense of persona, all strongly remind us that we must devote far more attention to Swift's inheritance as a poet than we have heretofore done. The second is that any individual poem by Swift is likely to reflect his poetic inheritance eccentrically: often simultaneously accepting, rejecting, denouncing, and absorbing its elements. As Thomas Gilmore suggests in his own very complex psychological interpretation of Swift's scatological verse, the truth is that Swift saw the human situation too many ways at once to allow himself *easy* certainties either of thought or of style. As a moral man he was compelled to make choices, and as a moralist he all his life defended the terms that make civilization possible. But he almost always knew what his defenses cost, and as a poet he remained remarkably open to the events that passed before his eyes, and to the thoughts and even dreams that passed between his mind and heart.

For over two centuries now, we have been so discomfited by this complicating breadth that we sought consistency even in the politician Swift, who began life as a Whig, lived it as a Tory, and continually deplored the idea of party itself. We sought such consistency, too, in the churchman Swift, who preached pamphlets in pulpit, prayed in private, always defended the Church, and sometimes doubted Christ's divinity.

And we sought consistency most in the poet Swift, in whom we encounter all the roles of Swift's long life. Times change, though. For example, sobered by the consequences of our own century's rigid ideologies, few of us today would read Swift's hilarious choice between the inside of things and their outsides in the "Digression concerning Madness" as anything except an outrageously false dichotomy. Not that we are better readers than our predecessors; it is just that our very times have taught us that only fools choose between absolute credulity and absolute curiosity, and only knaves offer such a choice. Questions about moral abstractions make sense in particular cases, but moral abstracts considered abstractly are both meaningless and dangerous.

Swift's verse is a canon of particular cases; that is its strength and chief delight. To reflect that particularity, the essays in this volume are arranged chronologically, not thematically. In these essays each of us has attempted to trace the pattern of Swift's thought as Swift worked himself through first this, then that occasion. If in our labors each of us has sometimes attempted to extrapolate from the poems too big a statement of the truth as Swift saw it, each of us has also been chastened by our colleagues' efforts. Jointly, we have learned to value more highly than ever the poetry of Jonathan Swift, greatest satirist and second poet of his age.

J.I.F.

Contemporary Studies
of Swift's Poetry

1

Swift on High Pindaric Stilts

DAVID SHEEHAN

State University of New York at Stony Brook

Until quite recently critics were just about unanimous in estimating the amount of critical attention Jonathan Swift's pindaric odes deserve: none. Deane Swift early declared Swift's pindarics "intirely out of the road of his talents," and that judgment generally prevailed.[1] In the last decade the odes have received more careful scrutiny as anticipations of Swift's more mature work, particularly in satire. At the heart of the "Ode to Sancroft," for example, Edward W. Rosenheim, Jr. finds "the practice of that art—call it satire or polemic rhetoric or merely the literature of attack—which has made Swift immortal."[2]

We can extend this critical appreciation of Swift's early odes by considering a further proposition. In addition to being studied as anticipations of the later works, Swift's poems are worth studying as pindaric odes in the context of other seventeenth-century pindarics. Specifically, I would argue that what some critics have seen as a struggle between Swift's personal satiric awareness and the panegyrical intention of the pindaric form is in fact not such a struggle, but rather Swift's contribution to a development in the seventeenth century that saw the pindaric turned to satiric as well as panegyric ends.

While it is true that Swift's predecessors and contemporaries regarded the ode as an essentially panegyric form,[3] it is also evident that Swift saw its satiric possibilities. Each of his pindarics is to some degree satiric, with highly specific attacks on James II and Louis XIV in the "Ode to the King," general attacks on "the Atheists of the Age" and others in the "Ode to the Athenian Society," and both general and specific attacks on political, intellectual, and religious targets in the "Ode to Sir William Temple" and the "Ode to Dr. William Sancroft." Some may be tempted to read Swift's final words to his muse in the ode to Sancroft—"Check in thy satire, angry muse,/Or a more worthy subject chuse"[4] (ll. 259-60)—as an attempt "to persuade himself that satire is essentially alien to the spirit of poetry,"[5] especially the pindaric, and to conclude that "Swift simply cannot accommodate Pindaric inventiveness and praise with his own essentially satiric awareness."[6] But this tendency to see Swift's use of satire in the pindarics as essentially his personal struggle with an inappropriate form should be corrected in light of the fact that the satiric pindaric is a discernible tradition within seventeenth-century British poetry, and that Swift was extending this tradition.

Ben Jonson's "Ode to Himselfe" is an early example of the satiric pindaric in the seventeenth century. Writing in response to the criticism of his play *The New Inn* in 1629, Jonson directed vituperation against the stage and the age:

> COme leave the loathed Stage,
> And the more loathsome Age,
> Where pride and impudence in faction knit,
> Usurpe the Chaire of wit.
>
> (ll. 1-4)

After describing his critics' swinish taste, Jonson invokes "Pindars fire" in the aid of satiric attack:

> Leave things so prostitute,
>   And take th' Alcaike Lute;
> Or thine own Horace, or Anacreons Lyre;
>   Warme thee by Pindars fire:
> And though thy Nerves be shrunke, and blood be cold,
>
> Ere years have made thee old,
>   Strike that disdainfull heat
>   Throughout, to their defeat:
> As curious fooles, and envious of thy straine,
> May blushing sweare, no Palsi's in thy braine.[7]
>
>   (ll. 41-50)

Charles Cotton is even more consistently satiric in his pindarics than Jonson. Taken together, Cotton's pindarics entitled "Hope," "Melancholy," "Woman," "Poverty," "Death," and "Contentment" make up a comprehensive satire against mankind. In the world of Cotton's odes the good person is surrounded by the malice and treachery of others, and the poverty-stricken man lives a life "measur'd out by fear" and pursued by "bloody Persecutors,/(Who formerly have been my suitors)."[8] In one of his most satiric pindarics Cotton describes the insatiable appetite that keeps man from real contentment:

> But 'tis our selves that give this frailty sway,
>   By our own promptness to obey
>   Our lust, pride, envy, avarice;
> By being so confederate with vice,
>   As to permit it to control
>   The rational immortal soul.

In Cotton's hands the ode was consistently turned from panegyric to satiric purposes, describing a world, as Rochester and Swift would later, as one in which "Man is Man's foe" and "brutes more civil are, and kind,/Than Man whose reason passions blind."

After Charles Cotton one of the great practitioners of the satiric ode in the seventeenth century was Samuel Butler, whose only three pindarics are all expressly satiric. Butler's "Upon an Hypocritical Nonconformist" is a pindaric satire directed against one of Swift's favorite targets, "Our modern self-willed Edifier,"

> That out of Things as far from Sense, and more,
>   Contrives new Light and Revelation,
>   The Creatures of th' Imagination,
>   To worship and fall down before;
>   Of which his crack'd Delusions draw
>   As monstrous Images and rude,
> As ever *Pagan*, to believe in, hew'd;
>   Or Madman in a Vision saw.[9]

Here is the pindaric turned to full satiric purposes. As Robert Thyer said in his note to the odes in his 1759 edition of Butler's *Genuine Remains*, "some Readers may perhaps think [the pindaric form] too grave and solemn for the Subject, and the turn of *Butler's* Wit. It must however be allow'd, that he falls no ways short of his usual Depth and Reach of Thought, Keenness of Satyr, and Acuteness of Expression."[10] That Butler found the form congenial is suggested by his success with two other pindaric satires, "Upon Modern Critics" and "To the Happy Memory of the most Renown'd Du-Val." The satire in the latter poem is directed against Claude Du-Val, a Frenchman born in Normandy who later became "a notorious Highwayman in *England;* and having been a brisk, smart, gay, and handsome Fellow, and of about Twenty-seven Years of Age, when he was hang'd at *Tyburn* (which was on the 21st of *January* 1669) did draw the Loves of many Females in *London* towards him."[11] The poem is a mock-panegyric ironically praising Du-Val as "A great

Example to Mankind" and as a "valiant" commander of forces against small tradesmen bringing cheese or malt or bacon to market:

> He made th' undaunted *Waggoner* obey,
> And the fierce *Higler* Contribution pay,
>   The savage *Butcher* and stout *Drover*
> Durst not to him their feeble Troops discover.[12]

Butler also takes advantage of his subject to satirize the French for their foolish obsession with fashions, the British for imitating the French, and the ladies for their infatuation with Du-Val.

In 1679 John Oldham contributed to the tradition of the satiric ode by appending to his *Satyrs upon the Jesuits* a pindaric ode that soon became known by the title "Satyr against Vertue."[13] This satiric ode is a paradoxical encomium meant, as Oldham states in his "Advertisement" to the 1685 edition of *Satyrs upon the Jesuits*, "to abuse those, who value themselves upon their Wit and Parts, in praising Vice; and to shew, that others of sober Principles, if they would take the same liberty in Poetry, could strain as high rants in Profaneness as they."[14] Throughout the poem Oldham attacks "Vertue! thou solemn grave impertinence,/Abhorr'd by all the Men of Wit, and Sense" (stanza 3). Although the irony in the poem is of the simplest kind, Oldham does use the pindaric form to achieve a special intensity in his description of the "great *Royal Society* of Vice,/Whose Talents are to make discoveries,/And advance Sin like other Arts and Sciences" (stanza 11). As Oldham says in his poetic "Apology for the foregoing Ode, by way of Epilogue," his ode was intended "not to flatter Vice, but to Traduce,"[15] and it is a significant contribution to the tradition of the seventeenth-century satiric pindaric.

The satiric impulse never entirely dominates any of Abra-

ham Cowley's odes, but it does find momentary expression in
the pindaric elegies on the deaths of William Hervey and Dr.
Scarborough, and in the odes "To the Royal Society" and
"To Mr. Hobs."[16] In the third stanza of the ode to Hobbes,
for example, Cowley describes the "out-worn" fields of
contemporary knowledge:

> The *Fields* which answer'd well the *Ancients Plow*,
> Spent and out-worn return no *Harvest* now,
> In barren *Age* wild and unglorious lie,
>   And boast of *past Fertilitie*,
> The *poor relief* of *Present Povertie*.

Like Cowley, Dryden used the pindaric form almost exclusively for panegyrics, but even he allowed the satirist's voice
to be raised in the pindaric elegy to the memory of Anne
Killegrew:

> O Gracious God! How far have we
> Prophan'd thy Heav'nly Gift of Poesy?
> Made prostitute and profligate the Muse,
> Debas'd to each obscene and impious use,
> Whose Harmony was first ordain'd Above
> For Tongues of Angels, and for Hymns of Love?
> O wretched We! why were we hurry'd down
>   This lubrique and adult'rate age,
>   (Nay added fat Pollutions of our own)
>   T' increase the steaming Ordures of the Stage?[17]

Another poet who, like Jonson, Cotton, and Butler,
turned the pindaric entirely toward satiric ends is Thomas
Otway. The subtitle of the one pindaric ode he wrote indicates this emphasis: "The Poet's Complaint of his Muse; or,
A Satyr Against Libells."[18] This ode is full-fledged allegorical
satire using a detailed account of the birth and vicious career
of Libell—"A Beast of Monstrous guise" (l. 246)—to describe

the origins, personalities, and activities of the Whig faction, from the rebellion and regicide of the 1640s, to the desolation of the Plague and Great Fire of 1665-66, to what Otway regarded as the malicious and treasonous Whig attacks that forced Charles II to ask James to leave England in 1679 at the height of the Popish Plot tensions. According to the dedicatory letter to the Earl of Ossory, Otway intended to "add a second part" to his poem, "and doe all those Great and Good men Justice, that have in his [James's] Calamities stuck fast to so gallant a Friend and so good a Master."[19] But this ode he reserved for satiric attack on those whose libels have "prophan'd/ With spurious Verse his spotless Fame" (ll. 552-53).

When we recognize the existence of the satiric ode as a minor tradition in the seventeenth century, and see the success some poets had with the form, we might be less apt to regard Swift's early odes as examples of an irreconcilable conflict between panegyric and satire, and more prepared to judge them for what they are—satiric pindarics. The implications of this perspective can be illustrated in terms of the least-often discussed of Swift's early pindarics, the "Ode to the King." As a purely panegyric ode, this poem is not entirely successful. The characterization of William III is remarkably abstract. The first two stanzas of the poem set forth a general principle, that "being *Great*" (l. 5) is an empty and ephemeral state unless it is linked to "the Delight of *Doing Good*" (l. 19). The third stanza applies this principle to William, not by characterizing the king in any personal detail, but by invoking that model of heroic virtue, Tamburlaine. Responsive as we are to Christopher Marlowe's willful and pitiless protagonist, Tamburlaine may seem an odd model of virtue and valor. But as in so many other instances in his early odes, Swift is here influenced by the writings of his patron, Sir William Temple. In his essay "Of Heroic Virtue" Temple offers an image of Tamburlaine that differs from Marlowe's, one that emphasizes not his power but his virtue. Temple describes Tamburlaine's continuing to honor his alliance with the Greek emperor at Constantinople who, free from Bajazet's tyranny, now lay at Tamburlaine's mercy: "Nothing was greater or more heroical in this victorious Tamerlane, than the faith and honour wherewith he observed this alliance with the Greeks." Temple summarizes Tamburlaine's character: "He was, without question, a great and heroic genius, of great justice, exact discipline, generous bounty, and much piety, adoring one God, though he was neither Christian, Jew, nor Mahometan, and deserves a nobler character than could be allowed by modern writers to any person of a nation so unlike themselves."[20] This is the alliance of virtue and greatness that Swift is praising in his poem, and that makes Tamburlaine an appropriate parallel to William. But it is also worth noting that William himself does not really appear in these first three stanzas. Even in the fourth stanza, which focuses on William's individual contribution to the victory at the battle of the Boyne, the "Destroying Angel" (l. 48) is the active force, not William. And in the fifth stanza William's domination of the "*Giddy British Populace*" (l. 72) and that "Discontented Brood" (l. 82), the Scots, is presented to us indirectly in terms of extended similes comparing William to Mercury charming Argus and to "some *Patrician* God" (l. 93) visiting the underworld.

The character of William, like the virtue he exemplifies, is in this ode abstract, ineffable, a powerful force beyond particularity. On the other hand, the targets of satire in this ode are presented in vivid particularity. Thus the "Scepter, Crown, and Ball" in the hands of a monarch without a moral sense becomes "Rattles for Infant Royalty to play withal." The "*Giddy British Populace*" (l. 72) is turned into a "Monster" (l. 79) with "many hundred eyes" (l. 78). The Scots are a bawling brood, "murmuring in *their Wilderness for Food*" (l. 87). James's justifications for his campaign against William are reduced to *"a rubbish Heap* of *broken Laws"* (l. 102), and James himself is reduced to a thoroughly material and deteriorating image of a dying candlewick:

> His scrap of Life is but a Heap of Miseries,
>   The Remnant of a falling Snuff,
>   Which hardly wants another puff,
> And needs must *stink* when e'er it dies.
> (ll. 107-10)

In the most powerful lines of the poem Swift attacks Louis XIV in language directly opposite to the abstractions used to characterize William. Louis is "That Tennis-Ball of Fate" (l. 121), a "Gilded Meteor" (l. 122) that "Took its first Growth and Birth/ From the worst Excrements of Earth" (ll. 126-27) and will "end as it began, in Vapour, Stink, and Scum" (l. 129). This is the language of satire, reducing the targets of attack to a deteriorating materiality, in contrast to the deified abstractions like virtue—and William—which remain "Contemporary to Eternity" (l. 26). Both the panegyric and the satire are charged by being brought close together.

Rather than arguing for an irreconcilable conflict between the satiric and panegyric intentions in this and the other pindaric odes of Swift, we should see that Swift has managed a mutually reinforcing merger of the major panegyrical function of the pindaric ode with the complementary minor tradition of the seventeenth-century satiric ode developed by Jonson, Cotton, Oldham, Butler, and Otway. This view not only permits us to take Swift's early odes for what they are— satiric pindarics—but also helps us to place Swift's poetry in its literary contexts. If, in the face of those critics from Swift's day to ours who have found the early odes consistently bad, this approach helps to raise our appreciation for Swift's early efforts in this most difficult kind of poetry, so much the better.

34 DAVID SHEEHAN

NOTES

1. *Essay upon the Life, Writings, and Character of Dr. Jonathan Swift* (London: Bathurst, 1755), p. 118. For other substantially negative judgments on Swift's early odes, see Thomas Sheridan, *The Life of the Rev. Dr. Jonathan Swift*, 2d ed. (London: Rivington et al., 1787), p. 13; Sir Walter Scott, *Life of Swift* (2d ed., 1824) in *Swift: The Critical Heritage*, ed. Kathleen Williams (New York: Barnes & Noble, 1970), p. 297; F. Elrington Ball, *Swift's Verse: An Essay* (London: J. Murray, 1929), chap. 2 entitled "Pindaric and Heroic Aberration"; Herbert Davis, *Jonathan Swift: Essays on his Satire and Other Studies* (1931; reprint ed. New York: Oxford University Press, 1964), p. 172; Ricardo Quintana, *The Mind and Art of Jonathan Swift* (London: Oxford University Press, 1936; rev. ed. 1953), pp. 29-44; and Maurice Johnson, *The Sin of Wit: Jonathan Swift as a Poet* (Syracuse, N.Y.: Syracuse University Press, 1950), pp. 1-6.

2. "Swift's *Ode to Sancroft:* Another Look," *Modern Philology* 73 (1976): S39. For other discussions of Swift's pindarics as anticipating his later satire, see Emile Pons, *Swift: Les Années de jeunesse et le "Conte du Tonneau"* (Strasbourg and Oxford: Oxford University Press, 1925), pp. 165-66; Irvin Ehrenpreis, *Swift: The Man, His Works and the Age* (Cambridge, Mass.: Harvard University Press, 1962), 1:109-31; Kathleen Williams, *Jonathan Swift and the Age of Compromise* (Lawrence, Kan.: University of Kansas Press, 1958), pp. 38-42; Kathryn Montgomery Harris, " 'Occasions so few' ": Satire as a Strategy of Praise in Swift's Early Odes," *Modern Language Quarterly* 31 (1970): 22-37; Robert W. Uphaus, "From Panegyric to Satire; Swift's Early Odes and *A Tale of a Tub*," *Texas Studies in Literature and Language* 13 (1971): 55-70; Nora Crow Jaffe, *The Poet Swift* (Hanover, N.H.: University Press of New England, 1977), pp. 61-74. For a thoughtful reading of Swift's early odes that does not value them primarily for what they anticipate of the later Swift, but rather as poems in which Swift comes to terms with the limitations inherent in the human condition, see John Irwin Fischer's *On Swift's Poetry* (Gainesville: University Presses of Florida, 1978), pp. 1-54.

3. See Harris, " 'Occasions so few,' " p. 23; and Norman Maclean's influential essay "From Action to Image: Theories of the Lyric in the Eighteenth Century" in *Critics and Criticism*, ed. R. S. Crane (Chicago: University of Chicago Press, 1952), pp. 408-60. For a brief and generally negative account of the Pindaric as a vehicle for satire see George N. Shuster, *The English Ode from Milton to Keats* (1940; reprint ed. Gloucester, Mass.: Peter Smith, 1964), pp. 129-30.

4. All quotations of Swift's poetry are from *The Poems of Jonathan Swift*, ed. Sir Harold Williams, 3 vols., 2d ed. (Oxford: Clarendon Press, 1958).

5. John Middleton Murry, *Jonathan Swift: A Critical Biography* (London: J. Cape, 1954), p. 34.

6. Uphaus, "From Panegyric to Satire," p. 60.

7. *The Complete Poetry of Ben Jonson*, ed. William B. Hunter, Jr. (New York: New York University Press, 1963), pp. 386, 388. See also two other satiric odes by Jonson, "An Ode To Himselfe" and the ode beginning "If Men, and tymes were nowe," pp. 159, 406.

8. *The Poems of Charles Cotton,* ed. John Beresford (London: Cobden Sanderson, 1923), pp. 210-11, 218, 220. For the other quotations from Cotton in this paragraph see pp. 227, 229.

9. *The Genuine Remains in Verse and Prose of Mr. Samuel Butler,* ed. R[obert] Thyer, 2 vols. (London: J. and R. Tonson, 1759), 1: 126.

10. Ibid., 1: 125.

11. Cited by Thyer from Wood's *Athenae* in ibid., 1: 146n.

12. *Genuine Remains,* 1: 152.

13. *The Works of Mr. John Oldham, Together with his Remains* (London: Joseph Hindmarsh, 1686), bk. 1, pp. 93-110.

14. Ibid., bk. 1, "Advertisement," n.p.

15. Ibid., bk. 1, p. 111.

16. Abraham Cowley, *Poems,* ed. A. R. Waller (Cambridge: Cambridge University Press, 1905), pp. 37, st. 18; 197, st. 1; 448, st. 2; and, cited in the text, 189, st. 3.

17. *The Poems and Fables of John Dryden,* ed. James Kinsley (London: Oxford University Press, 1962), p. 346.

18. *The Works of Thomas Otway,* ed. J. C. Ghosh, 2 vols. (Oxford: Clarendon Press, 1932; reprint ed. 1968), 2: 401.

19. Ibid., 2: 403-4.

20. *The Works of Sir William Temple,* 4 vols. (London: J. Clarke et al., 1757), 3: 349-50. For a discussion of Temple's description of Tamburlaine and for an earlier sympathetic account in Richard Knolles's *The General Historie of the Turkes* (1603), see Donald B. Clark, "The Source and Characterization of Nicholas Rowe's *Tamerlane,*" *Modern Language Notes* 65 (1950): 145-52.

2

Swift and the Tradition of Informal Satiric Poetry

DONNA G. FRICKE

Bowling Green State University

Swift's satiric intention was always the same—to persuade his reader to stand before the mirror of satire and to see there the human form stripped of pretension, the fallen soul in need of reform and salvation. There is nothing unusual about this intention; it is common to all Christian satirists. What is unusual about Swift, especially among Augustan satirists, is his ready utilization of both prose and poetry. While we have come to accept his satiric poetry as an important complement to his prose satire, we have yet to appreciate the verse within the modes and traditions in which it is written.

Unlike Dryden and Pope, who chose to write within the classical formal mode, Swift wrote satiric poetry in the informal or colloquial mode. Swift's choice, too, has classical precedent, but unlike the formal mode, the informal has roots that run deep in English literature. Swift's choice permitted him to reach toward a larger constituency than Dryden and Pope wrote for, and to approach that constituency in a different manner. As we know, Swift sometimes read his verse to his cook.

The technical differences between formal and informal manners are manifold, but the difference in feel is easy to suggest. For example, whether one reads "Verses on the Death of Dr. Swift" as a standard satirist's apology or as a meditation on death, one cannot but be struck by the contrast between it and Pope's more classically formal apology, "Epistle to Dr. Arbuthnot." In place of the interrupting interlocutor of formal apology, one finds indifferent friends and misinformed strangers in a pub responding to the news of the poet's life and death. Without pretensions or idealistic expectations or self-conscious literary imitation, Swift tells us what will be said of him after his death, adds some sharp comments of his own, and leaves us to make of his poem what we can or will. His poem strips away our resistances and engages us in what Henry W. Sams has termed "satire of the second person."[1] Informal communication, directed to "you," "reader," the poem is conveyed through colloquial forms and conversational poetic meters. Virgil and Homer never talked like this, but Chaucer, Skelton, and Butler did.

Not long ago Irvin Ehrenpreis reminded us that the point of formal satiric poetry is sometimes blunted by its very beauty.[2] Years ago classical scholar J. Wright Duff said the same thing the other way around: "What gives satire its vital importance in Latin literature is not poetic charm . . . it is rather its faithful representation of contemporary life and its comments thereupon."[3] Although often ignored as such, there is a long tradition in English literature of this satiric "faithful representation of contemporary life." Poems in this tradition are not often beautiful because they do not aim at beauty. But neither are they aesthetically dull; they court purity, understood as the rough simplicity of an earlier age.

Significant of his membership among the seekers of an earlier simplicity, Swift chose to specialize in the octosyllabic, rather than the heroic, couplet. The octosyllabic couplet was known to English readers through classical and continental influences on the literature: it was a common measure of accentual Latin hymns and was popularized in secular narrative literature by way of medieval French poetry and the twelfth-century Anglo-Norman poets like Wace. But it also has an older English past when viewed as an offspring of Old English poetry with its four points of emphasis, and it had become a common structure for Anglo-Saxon narratives, probably because of its singsong rapid movement that lends itself so well to narrative verse. So the octosyllabic couplet, argues Elbert N. S. Thompson in a rare essay on the subject, seems to be more indigenous to English than the heroic and less dominated by principles of Italian metrics.[4]

In an age beginning to emphasize its national literature and concerned to standardize and purify the English language, Swift chose, against a more elitist critical current, an indigenous English form. Perhaps he did not think of his choice in these terms, but they are consonant with the linguistic conservatism he exhibited all of his life. Then, too, after his own fashion Swift always was a patriot. His choice of forms reflects some of his deepest traits; writing octosyllabics, he tells us who he is. But, because forms have histories, his choice of forms also affected his type of poetry. When Swift took up the octosyllabic, the form had a long, well-developed history in English lyric and narrative verse. Both Chaucer (*House of Fame* and *The Book of the Duchess*) and the *Owl and the Nightingale* poet had used the form very effectively to produce narrative flow through run-on lines and feminine endings. In lyric use, the Elizabethan song writers had excelled with the form. Breaking the octosyllabic couplets into short stanzas (often only four lines), they achieved a simplicity of expression rather than the narrative continuity of medieval literary use. Campion and Herrick were especially good in this mode, and Marvell was able to combine their effective lyric expression with the narrative flow of the medieval poets. Because all this had happened, Swift found himself able to use his favorite poetic form for narratives, lyrics (especially the poems for Stella), and biting satire.

Of course, his immediate poetic forefather in the use of the octosyllabic is Samuel Butler, in the satiric-ironic narrative *Hudibras*. What Swift builds on is Butler's rhyming innovations, which enhance the possibilities of the less-inflected, modern English language of the Restoration period. Swift found even greater variety possible in the octosyllabic rhymed couplet by varying the regular masculine rhyme with the addition of a permissible feminine syllable or with the multiple-word rhyme typical of the Hudibrastic. He also learned from Butler a way to control the irony of deflating the pompous hero or heroine through vivid narrative description. To see what Swift does and does not owe Butler, we can compare a six-line section from Canto 1 of Part 1 of *Hudibras* with the opening of Swift's "Prometheus, A Poem":

Hudibras[5]

> When *Gospel-trumpeter,* surrounded
> With long-ear'd rout, to Battel sounded,
> And Pulpit, Drum Ecclesiastick,
> Was beat with fist, instead of a stick:
> Then did Sir *Knight* abandon dwelling,
> And out he rode a Colonelling.
>> (ll. 9–14)

"Prometheus, A Poem"[6]

> When first the 'Squire and *Tinker Wood*
> Gravely consulting *Ireland's* Good,
> Together mingl'd in a Mass
> Smith's *Dust,* and *Copper, Lead* and *Brass,*
> The Mixture thus by Chymick Art,
> United close in ev'ry part.
> In Fillets roll'd, or cut in Pieces,

Appear'd like one continu'd Spec'es
And by the forming Engine struck,
On all the same IMPRESSION stuck.
(ll. 1–10)

Or we can consider two additional Hudibrastics from "Van-brug's House":

Van, (for 'tis fit the Reader know it)
Is both a Herald and a Poet.
(ll. 59–60)

So, Modern Rhymers strive to blast
The Poetry of Ages past,
Which having wisely overthrown,
They from it's Ruins build their own.
(ll. 89–92)

In both instances we see that the multiple rhymes, popularized by Butler, are frequently used by Swift. But we also see that there is a great deal more variety in Swift's octosyllabics than in Butler's. Clarence L. Kulischek put the case well at the conclusion to his article "Swift's Octosyllabics and the Hudibrastic Tradition": "in poems such as the best of the addresses to Stella, Swift's octosyllabics are to the Hudibrastic couplet what the blank verse of *Tamburlaine* was to that of *Gorboduc*."[7] Swift's contemporaries knew this truth, too, and paid him the ultimate compliment of imitation. Oliver Goldsmith's "New Simile, in the Manner of Swift" is an attempt to capture Swift's own mingling of the rough octosyllabic couplet with neoclassical requirements of a harmonious style. So, more strikingly, is Pope's "The Seventh Epistle of the First Book of Horace, Imitated in the Manner of Dr. Swift."[8]

Scatter your Favours on a Fop,
Ingratitude's the certain crop;
And 'tis but just, I'll tell you wherefore,

> You give the things you never care for.
> A wise man always is or should
> Be mighty ready to do good;
> But makes a diff'rence in his thought
> Betwixt a Guinea and a Groat.
>
> (ll. 31–38)

Interestingly, when Swift and Pope collaborated on another octosyllabic, "Horace, Part of the Sixth Satire of the Second Book Imitated," Swift was displeased with the result. Pope's purity is of a different order from his friend's—quite useless in Swift's metier.

In general, then, Swift's satiric use of the octosyllabic is both built upon and compares favorably with the accomplishments in the same meter of Chaucer, Butler, Marvell, and anonymous seventeenth-century court poets. His octosyllabic lyrics, notably those to Stella, are as successful as those of Lodge, Jonson, Herrick, Lovelace, and Marvell. Therefore Swift's favoring of the octosyllabic, rather than the heroic, couplet should not be viewed as his peculiar aberration or be compared only with Butler's work. Swift incorporates Butler's narrow use of the form and goes far beyond him in demonstrating its versatility.

In fact, among the earlier writers of colloquial satire, it is probably John Skelton who most reminds one of Swift, for between these two the similarities are striking. To an eminent degree both poets share what Duff termed the "vital importance" of satire, its ability to comment effectively on the realistic condition of contemporary society. Also, Swift and Skelton share a unique English satiric thrust—the priest's bold attack on corruption in the church and state alike, and the poet's concern for the effectiveness and development of his native language. Finally, both writers experimented with satiric poetic forms in an effort to find a satisfactory poetic vehicle and both were frustrated in their ecclesiastical careers because of their outspokenness.

What has been described as "Angry Skelton's breathless rimes" is a verse form devised by Skelton (derived from Latin rhymed prose) to convey his spirited satiric attacks. Stanley Fish writes that at line 321 of *Colyn Cloute* Skelton "climaxes a description of the Bishops' addiction to luxury with a couplet that anticipates Butler and Swift in its force and conciseness"[9]:

> Theyr moyles golde dothe eate,
> Theyr neyghbours dye for meate.[10]
>   (ll. 321–22)

And Skelton's "Elynour Rummyng," which has been described as a verbal painting, represents yet another typical aspect of informal verse satire that Swift specialized in—the grotesque portrait:

> Her lewde lyppes twayne,
> They slauer, men sayne,
> Lyke a ropy rayne,
> A gummy glayre:
> She is ugly fayre;
> Her nose somdele hoked,
> And camously croked,
> Neuer stoppynge,
> But euer droppynge;
> Her skynne lose and slacke;
> Grained lyke a sacke;
> With a croked backe.
>   (ll. 22–33)

These conjunctions are natural. Swift and Skelton both wrote in periods of literary as well as political and ecclesiastical turmoil. The battle over the relationship between poetry and rhetoric was being waged with as much vehemence as the battle over old and new domestic order. Stephen Hawes, Skelton's literary enemy, had declared English an inadequate vehicle for the expression of fine ideas and wanted a return to classical rhetoric (the five classical divisions). Swift's enemies were more numerous. Swift and the other Scriblerians fought against the Grub Street hacks and the incompetent poets laureate of the Georgian reign, and Swift more blatantly than the rest by devising his own version of Skeltonic defiance. But in a sense his revolt was also against the classical couplet of Dryden and his friend Pope. As W. K. Wimsatt puts it: "the short couplet in its laughing mode was something broader and coarser, distinctly late Latin, vernacular, and anti-classical. It was a revolt against and a vagabond swerve away from the ancient decorum." Later, Wimsatt sums up the tradition: "Rhyme in the Goliardic-Skeltonic-Scarronian-Hudibrastic tradition is all that Gothic, rude, and beggarly jingle deplored by such civilized theorists as Campion, Milton, and Roscommon. In that short-couplet tradition Swift found his own voice, his characteristic freedom and crashing energy. Thwarted *Episcopus,* actual *Decanus,* Swift was an Augustan *Archipoeta Redivivus.*"[11]

Finally, though, we probably should not consider Swift's chosen poetic form as simply a rhetorical revolt, for the poetic vehicle also carried a good deal of the same serious satiric message to be found in Horatian colloquial verse. Here Swift's immediate poetic predecessor is not so much Butler, whose satiric focus was narrow, as Rochester, who also displayed Swift's concern with a broad range of activity that conveyed an often-ignored ethical significance, or as his seventeenth-century counterpart, political satirist Andrew Marvell, who also needs to be investigated as a part of this English tradition. David Farley-Hills argues that Marvell is the most distinguished political poet of the Restoration and that his "contribution to English verse satire has been grossly under-rated." And later, in a discussion of Suckling's "Upon My Lady Carlisle's Walking in Hampton Court Garden," Farley-Hills draws an important parallel between Suckling's tone and the poetry of Swift: "This is poetry of negative vision we meet frequently in the Restoration and in Swift, whose special characteristic as a poet it is. . . . The desire to strip off surface 'unreality' (a familiar theme in Swift) leads to a suggestion of a disparity between the apparent and the real."[12] Thus there are several, and these are only a few examples, satiric poets immediately preceding Swift who need to be reexamined in this broader colloquial English satiric tradition, who share his poetic concerns, and, frequently, his poetic style. "Strictly speaking," Austin Clark writes, "Swift really belongs, both in his temperament and his writings, to the seventeenth century, which is still neglected."[13] But it is not so much that he belongs to the seventeenth century rather than the eighteenth as that he belongs to a satiric tradition that differs from that of Dryden and Pope. If we include his prose satire, we must consider him *the* major satirist of the Augustan period, but even on the merits of his verse satire he deserves a place beside Dryden and Pope as the Augustan Archpoet, an Augustan English reviver of the medieval satiric tradition.

That Pope was aware of, and perhaps even a little envious of, the popular response to the English informal satiric verse tradition is evident in these lines from "Epistle to Augustus":

> It is the rust we value, not the gold,
> Chaucer's worst ribaldry is learn'd by rote,
> And beastly Skelton Heads of Houses quote.
> (ll. 37–39)

Indeed, there is no need to apologize for Swift's kind of satiric poetry. It is part of a long and effective classical and English informal satiric tradition. And it is memorable.

NOTES

1. "Swift's Satire of the Second Person," *English Literary History* 26 (1959): 36-44.

2. *Literary Meaning and Augustan Values* (Charlottesville: University Press of Virginia, 1974), see especially pp. 63-75.

3. *Roman Satire: Its Outlook on Social Life* (Berkeley: University of California Press, 1936), p. 6.

4. "The Octosyllabic Couplet," *Philological Quarterly* 18 (1939): 257-68.

5. All quotations of Butler's *Hudibras* are from *Hudibras*, ed. John Wilder (Oxford: Clarendon Press, 1967).

6. All quotations of Swift's poetry are from *The Poetry of Jonathan Swift*, ed. Sir Harold Williams, 3 vols., 2d ed. (Oxford: Clarendon Press, 1958).

7. *Journal of English and Germanic Philology* 53 (1954): 368.

8. All quotations of Pope's poetry are from *Poems of Alexander Pope*, ed. John Butt (New Haven, Conn.: Yale University Press, 1963).

9. *John Skelton's Poetry* (New Haven, Conn.: Yale University Press, 1965), p. 184.

10. All quotations of Skelton's poetry are from *Skelton's Poetical Works*, ed. Alexander Dyce, 2 vols. (London: Thomas Rodd, 1843).

11. "Rhetoric and Poems: The Example of Swift," in *The Author in His Work: Essays on a Problem in Criticism*, ed. Louis L. Martz and Aubrey Williams (New Haven, Conn.: Yale University Press, 1978), pp. 231–32.

12. *The Benevolence of Laughter: Comic Poetry of the Commonwealth and Restoration* (London: Macmillan, 1974), pp. 3, 38.

13. "The Poetry of Swift," in *Jonathan Swift, 1667-1967: A Dublin Tercentenary Tribute,* ed. Roger McHugh and Philip Edwards (Dublin: Dolmen, 1967), p. 97.

3

Swift's Poetry and the Gentle Reader

ARTHUR H. SCOUTEN

The University of Pennsylvania

Swift's poems were indeed intended for "the gentle reader," for the Romantic notion of literature as self-expression had not yet arisen. However, the poems were not composed for everyone to read, and we need to remember the different classes or categories of audiences that the Dean had in mind for different poems. First, there are those which Swift approved for publication and which were intended for the general public. Second, there is the large body of occasional verse designed for a specific, private audience, such as Sir William Temple and his sister, or the household of Lord Berkeley, or light verse to be read at the dinner table to Esther Johnson, or the Grattans, or at Market Hill for the delectation of Sir Arthur Acheson and his relatives, or even a *jeu d'esprit* written with his left hand for Thomas Sheridan.

Even in his public poems, Swift thought in terms of an intended audience, and he established several categories. In 1733 he evaluated Pope's epitaph on Gay with relation to the "Vulgar Readers," in contrast to the customary readers of

Pope's poetry.[1] In praising another poem by Pope, he writes of its success with "the best Judges" in Dublin.[2] However, he observes in regard to the "Epistle to Bathurst" that parts of that poem were not too clear to "midling Readers."[3] Thus, we can find semiliterate, middling, and sophisticated readers, as well as London readers and Dubliners. From these categories we can conjecture that even an obviously public poem like "Traulus" (1730), a witty dialogue concerned with Lord Allen's attempt to bring about a prosecution of Swift and his printer, was probably designed for the less-sophisticated Dublin reading public.

Swift's concern with differentiating between public poems and those amusing trifles intended for private audiences is shown in both the contents and the publication history of volume 2 of the authorized edition of his works by Faulkner in 1735. Most of the private poems are excluded, and thus this volume contains only about half of Swift's poetry. We know from Williams, Davis, and Teerink that Swift read page proof for this volume, and made numerous changes. In addition, a recently discovered set of Faulkner's edition of 1735, now in the English Faculty Library at Oxford, shows that Swift excised four poems after the book had been printed. This set, which has fortunately survived, can be termed the first *state* of the edition. Volume 2 contains the four poems that are deleted from later issues of this edition, and the twenty-seven leaves of cancels are bound in at the end of the volume.[4] One of the deletions was "Traulus," and Swift probably withdrew it because its subject was local Dublin politics and not of wide interest.

From these examples of Swift's control over publication of the poems in the Faulkner edition of 1735, where we find the poetry that the Dean chose for exposure to the general reader, we can proceed to his correspondence for more illustrations of his practice of dividing his readers into various categories. To Pope, Swift described certain Market Hill poems as to be read only to the Achesons and their relatives or to friends; he adds that when "The Journal of a Dublin Lady" was sent off for publication, he deleted the lines about the Acheson family.[5] In another letter Swift mentions some occasional verse as "never intended for publick view."[6] Indeed, one version of "Epistle to a Lady" does not contain the political passages. That Swift thought primarily in terms of an audience is clearly documented in many of his letters to Pope and Bolingbroke.[7]

With special reference to this light verse written for designated private groups, two recent trends in modern Swift scholarship, one of omission and one of commission, are most unfortunate, and deserve careful scrutiny. In an important review-article, George Sherburn years ago warned that "no book on Swift has ever done justice to the infinite playfulness of his mind."[8] Fortunately, some books and essays on Swift since 1938 have shown an awareness of this playfulness; nevertheless, a few biographers and literary historians still present the old view of the gloomy Dean. The best corrective to this erroneous estimate is the bagatelles. If F. R. Leavis and David Daiches had read these unauthorized skits and riddles and occasional verses that Swift rejected from his published works, they would be less likely to call the Dean a proponent of negativism or speak of his "natural misanthropy."[9] Biographers of Swift should read every scrap of Swift's writing and become familiar with these bagatelles before they start to pass judgment on the Dean himself.

The second error is to take these minor, playful pieces and praise them for their artistic merit and high seriousness. The business of overrating occasional poems written for a specific private audience (whether he authorized publication or not) does a disservice to Swift studies, especially at a time when we are witnessing a revival of interest in his poetry. In a recent essay, for example, one writer singles out the poem "Stella's Birth-Day, A great Bottle of Wine, long buried, being that

Day dug up" (1723) for high praise, and quotes the following extract:

> First, nine Ways looking, let her stand
> With an old Poker in her Hand;
> Let her describe a Circle round
> In *Saunder's* Cellar on the Ground:
> A Spade let prudent *Archy* hold,
> And with Discretion dig the Mould:
> Let *Stella* look with watchful Eye,
> *Rebecca, Ford* and *Grattans* by.[10]
>
> (ll. 53-60)

The critic tells us that the verse is "excellent," and further claims that in this poem "art and life fuse," and that "life becomes art, and art becomes life."[11] Swift has indeed presented a convivial domestic scene, but the language of the presentation is doggerel. The rhythm is monotonous, poetic diction abounds, and one wonders whether there are any circles that are not round. If this is good poetry, what terminology does the critic reserve for "On Poetry: A Rapsody" or "Verses on the Death of Dr. Swift?" And besides, what experienced reader of poetry is going to be convinced by the assertion that the verse is "excellent?" Also, the grandiloquent formulation of "life/art; art/life" seems pretentious. The author of these phrases should reflect on the fact that Dean Swift spent many years collecting such expressions for his satiric opus *Polite Conversation*.

Despite the contributions of such important scholars as Claude Rawson, Maurice Johnson, and David Vieth to this new interest in Swift's poetry, old prejudices against the Augustan concept of what is true poetry still persist. A significant item in this connection appears in a recent collection of Clark Seminar papers given during 1973-74. After Claude Rawson concluded his essay on Swift, Baudelaire, and

Eliot, Novak refers to a lengthy discussion by members of the audience, focused on whether a case could be made for saying that Swift was an important poet.[12] A considerable number of specialists in English and American literature were interested enough in the topics and speakers to engage in a discussion of the importance of Swift's poetry. But Novak reports that at least one of those involved was evidently not ready to accept Swift as a major poet. If an audience for the William Andrews Clark lectures is any kind of reliable index or reflection of our colleagues in the profession, we should probably be on guard against overestimating Swift's verse, especially the playful poems intended for private consumption.

Still another kind of problem appears in the occasional poem called "The Journal."[13] Swift probably composed this piece in the fall of 1721, during an extended visit at Gaulston House, a seat of the Rochfort family. The entire poem abounds in obscure details. How does "Heteroclit" Dan spoil a text (l. 24)? What is "*Dragon* rowes" [Williams's note is inconclusive] (l. 23), or "dose away his Beef" (l. 40)? How does George ride "o'er the *Dragon*" (ll. 85, 92)?—a name revised and corrected in Faulkner's edition of 1737. These and other terms in this piece of humorous light verse are obviously "in-jokes," intelligible to members of the Rochfort family, accustomed to communicating through coded references. Using a poem replete with these cryptic and private meanings as a basis for a serious analysis of Swift's poetry can be a risky undertaking, the consequences of which may be seen in a recent essay by Aubrey Williams, in which he interprets this poem without being certain of numerous references.[14] Since he is unable to identify many of these allusions, he is forced to repeat the words "seems" or "may seem" seven times on pages 231-33 (when he reaches his explanation of the poem), together with such variants as "may simply be claiming" and "perhaps also claiming."

By way of contrast, let us look at a poem written at Market

Hill, "An Epistle to a Lady." Begun in 1730, it was revised, polished, and expanded until it reached a level of universal application, whereupon Swift sent it over to London by the Pilkingtons to be printed. We need know nothing about Lady Acheson to understand the poem. Swift writes of her:

> Thus, I find it by Experiment,
> Scolding moves you less than Merriment.
> I may storm and rage in vain;
> It but stupifies your Brain.
> But, with Raillery to nettle,
> Set your thoughts upon their Mettle:
> Gives Imagination Scope,
> Never lets your Mind elope:
> Drives out Brangling and Contention,
> Brings in Reason and Invention.
>   (ll. 207–16)

During conversation at the homes of his acquaintances or when he was host to his guests, Swift amused himself and delighted the assemblage with absurd, invented personae, in-jokes, puns, and sometimes with sharp raillery in the praise-by-blame vein. It was sophisticated play to make the farce of life go down, as a character says in Thomas Shadwell's *The Squire of Alsatia*. From Mrs. Pilkington, Delany, Deane Swift, and Sheridan, we learn how much Swift's friends enjoyed hearing these private, occasional poems and being entertained by his role-playing. We also know how people such as Sir Andrew Fountaine, for example, sought after the manuscripts of these poems.[15] But recent critics offer a contrary view, asserting that these gentle readers did not understand Swift's harsh jesting and railing techniques,[16] or that "evidence indicates that Swift offended Lady Acheson and her friends."[17] Yet we know that after Lady Acheson left her husband and moved to Dublin she continued in Swift's circle, and that there was a cordial exchange between them in later years after the Market Hill period.

That great repository of information about Swift—
Williams's edition of the correspondence—provides a passage
capable of quelling a variety of heresies and demonstrating an
appreciation of Swift's style by one "gentle reader." It was
written to Swift by Lady Johnson, an aunt of Sir Arthur
Acheson. She was one of several members of Sir Arthur's
family who had been regaled at Market Hill by Swift's reading
his poems:

(March 30, 1729)

Hon^d S^r

    I am a Huckster and Lives in *Strand Street* & has
Dealings with Several familys, a saterday Night a Case of
Instruments was sent me in pawn by a Certain person in
Marys Street for two Rowls a print of Butter four Herrings
and three Nagins of strong Waters, my foster brother who
ply's about that End of the town tells Me he wanst saw it in
your hand, fearing Hawkins's whip I send it to you and
will take an Other Course to gett My Money, so I remain
yours Hon^rs/Humble Sarv^t to Command/Martha Sharp.[18]

This amusing message was received and endorsed by Swift
with the annotation, "The best letter I ever read." As we look
back today on this letter and the endorsement, we find that
the Dean and his gentle reader were in perfect communion. In
the figure of "Martha Sharp," Lady Johnson, affecting appropriate vulgarity and backward grammar, has invented a
persona, a Dublin huckster and pawnbroker. Martha lives on
Strand Street (now Capel Street), at that time a shabby part of
town. The person pawning the case of instruments lives on
"Marys Street," more properly St. Mary's Abbey, but now
also named Capel Street.[19] However, it is the "Case of
Instruments" that is the object of our interest. Deane Swift
annotates it as a gift from Lady Johnson to Swift, but Irvin
Ehrenpreis objects to this identification because the case had
been seen in Swift's hand and therefore could not be a gift.
Ehrenpreis suggests a box of writing instruments. Other

specialists I consulted were at a complete loss for an identification.[20]

However, from the ample fund of his knowledge of eighteenth-century Dublin, Donald Torchiana makes the fascinating suggestion that the "Instruments" were for torture.[21] Now, torture had been abolished in England in 1688, by an order in council by James II. The last person for whom torture was ordered by the British government was the Roman Catholic playwright Henry Nevil Payne, who was tortured with thumbscrews in Scotland in 1702.[22] In 1708 an order in council extended the prohibition of torture to Scotland, but this ruling, like a number of other reforms, had not been made applicable to Ireland.[23]

Not every jailor knew how to torture; instead, one jailor was trained in the techniques, and when the warden of a prison needed to have someone tortured, this one particular jailor was summoned, perhaps a mordant eighteenth-century version of our familiar "have case; will travel!" We find further confirmation of these connections from the reference to Hawkins in Lady Johnson's letter. John Hawkins was at that time the chief jailor or warden of Newgate Prison in Dublin. Consequently, Lady Johnson would hardly have used his name as a symbol for justice or authority, and the allusion to the "Case of Instruments" in connection with Hawkins implies some relation to the prison of which he was the keeper. John T. Gilbert's *A History of the City of Dublin* reveals that the term *instruments* was often used in connection with the prison. A record of official payment goes as follows:

> Memorandum, that these bene the instruments of Iryn boght vpon Tresory costes and delured to (three bailliffs of the city of Dublin): In primis, iij sheres, ij kyves, ij Boltes . . .j Bolte with iij poyntes for mens handes, iij shaglis . . . ij yeokys . . . v pair maniclis.[24]

The secret is out! Since the "foster brother" once saw the case in Swift's *hand*, Lady Johnson appears to be accusing the Dean of torturing people with his satires. This charge is most interesting, especially for a satirist notoriously skeptical about the impact of satire. Not that Swift's satires are worth much: in the harsh world of Dublin pawnbrokers, they were valued at only "two Rowls a print of Butter four Herrings and three Nagins of strong Waters." Lady Johnson indulges herself in the exercise of one of Swift's favorite techniques: harsh raillery in the praise-by-blame tradition. And I submit the letter both as testimony that Lady Johnson, the author, must have understood the little jokes in Swift's poems, and as warning to those critics who attempt to delve into and understand Swift's public and private verse without considering the biobibliographical contexts of the poetry.

NOTES

1. *The Correspondence of Jonathan Swift*, ed. Sir Harold Williams (Oxford: Clarendon Press, 1965), 4: 133. Hereafter cited as *Corr.*

2. Ibid., 4: 134–35.

3. These distinctions were noted in Archibald C. Elias's Yale dissertation, *Jonathan Swift and Letter-Writing: The Natural and the Playful in His Personal Correspondence* (1974), pp. 161–62.

4. Full details are in Margaret Weedon, "An Uncancelled Copy of the First Collected Edition of Swift's Poems," *The Library*, 5th ser., 22 (1967): 44–56.

5. *Corr.*, 3: 312–14.

6. Ibid., 4: 26–29. As proof that the poems were not meant for the public, note that Swift cites "the careless ways of handling."

7. See, for example, *Corr.*, 3: 373, where Swift mentions the importance of audience, especially for letter writers.

8. "Methods in Books about Swift," *Studies in Philology* 35 (1938): 644.

9. Leavis regularly expressed a derogatory estimate; see *Revaluation: Tradition and Development in English Poetry* (London: Chatto & Windus, 1948), pp. 110–11; also "The Irony of Swift," in *Swift: A Collection of Critical Essays*, ed. Ernest Tuveson (Englewood Cliffs, N.J.: Prentice-Hall, 1964), p. 21; for Daiches, see *A Critical History of English Literature* (New York: Ronald Press, 1960), 2: 608.

10. All quotations of the poetry are from *The Poems of Jonathan Swift*, ed. Sir Harold Williams, 3 vols., 2d ed. (Oxford: Clarendon Press, 1958).

11. David Sheehan, "Swift's Social Verse and Political Poetry." Paper read at the 1977 MLA Special Session on Swift's Poetry.

12. *English Literature in the Age of Disguise*, ed. Maximillian Novak (Berkeley: University of California Press, 1977), p. 10.

13. See *Poems*, 1: 276–83.

14. "Swift and the Poetry of Allusion: 'The Journal,' " in *Literary Theory and Structure: Essays in Honor of William K. Wimsatt*, ed. Frank Brady, John Palmer, and Martin Price (New Haven, Conn.: Yale University Press, 1973), pp. 227–43.

15. Peter J. Croft, *Autograph Poetry in the English Language* (New York: McGraw-Hill, 1973), 1: 62.

16. Geoffrey Hill, "Jonathan Swift: the Poetry of 'Reaction,' " in *The World of Jonathan Swift: Essays for the Tercentenary*, ed. Brian Vickers (Cambridge, Mass.: Harvard University Press, 1968), pp. 202–3.

17. Nora Crow Jaffe, *The Poet Swift* (Hanover, N.H.: University Press of New England, 1977), p. 130.

18. *Corr.*, 3: 327.

19. C. T. M'Cready, *Dublin Street Names* (Dublin, 1892), pp. 64, 129.

20. In a personal letter from Ehrenpreis; also in a personal letter from Bernard Richards of Brasenose College. Richards finds reference to a running correspondence between 18 February 1728 and 19 November 1730 with John Gay over Swift's eating habits when dining with "the great." Swift defended himself with the excuse that poor poets can only afford bidentine forks, and one will then use the knife improperly. If Swift shared his correspondence with the Market Hill group, Richards contends, Lady Johnson might be sending some tridentine cutlery in a case.

21. During a telephone conversation and through subsequent supporting evidence noted here.

22. See *D.N.B.* s.v. Payne.

23. See *The Eighteenth Century*, ed. Alfred Corban (New York: McGraw-Hill, 1969), p. 291.

24. (Dublin, 1854), 1: 257–58.

4

Metaphors and Metamorphoses: Basic Techniques in the Middle Period of Swift's Poetry, 1698-1719

DAVID M. VIETH

Southern Illinois University, Carbondale

It is by now a commonplace that many of Swift's poems written from 1698 through 1719—for example, "The Story of Baucis and Philemon," "Vanbrug's House," and the two "Description" poems—depict mock-Ovidian metamorphoses or mock-Christian miracles.[1] Less often noted is the circumstance that extended metaphors, used in a manner that would strike most readers as outrageously unorthodox, occur with at least equal frequency, and sometimes equal brilliance, in this same group of poems—most obviously, in "The Description of a Salamander," "The Virtues of Sid Hamet the Magician's Rod," "The Fable of Midas," and "The Progress of Beauty."[2] The two techniques are not separate. Each involves, in intention at least, a eucharistic transformation of the bread and wine of life into the body and blood of art, which may be triumphantly successful on the part of the poet, or hilariously unsuccessful on the part of his subjects, or—ideally—both at once.

A simple example, relatively speaking, of an Ovidian metamorphosis or Christian miracle that changes nothing is Swift's "A Description of the Morning."[3] The miracle parodied in this debased dawn-piece is the divine fiat "Let there be light," which created the Garden of Eden. Instead of the order and purity of Eden, however, Swift's poem depicts the shabby, dimly lit, dirty (in both physical and moral senses) milieu of early eighteenth-century London, striving halfheartedly to restore order and cleanliness:

> The Slipshod Prentice from his Masters Door,
> Had par'd the Dirt, and Sprinkled round the Floor.
> Now *Moll* had whirl'd her Mop with dext'rous Airs,
> Prepar'd to Scrub the Entry and the Stairs.
> The Youth with Broomy Stumps began to trace
> The Kennel-Edge, where Wheels had worn the Place.[4]
>
> (ll. 5-10)

Despite the discrepancy between the vehicle and the tenor of the implied metaphor—that is, between the dingy, worn-down condition of London and the pastoral re-creation of the Golden Age in the Garden of Eden—traces of order and vitality remain in Swift's fallen city. There is life, akin to the vitality of Frances Harris and Mary the Cook-Maid, in the way Moll twirls her mop "with dext'rous Airs," and the events enumerated in the poem are ticked off in precise chronological order. There is even the daily miracle of the sun (certainly the sun; possibly the Son) having risen. Thus tenor and vehicle are not totally disjunctive.

Similar to the mock-pastoral of "A Description of the Morning" is the mock-georgic of Swift's "A Description of a City Shower," a "how-to-do-it" poem that begins appropriately by offering "sure Prognosticks" of an approaching downpour, in imitation of Virgil's *Georgics,* Book 1. Allusion is made to Noah's Flood (secondarily, to Deucalion's Flood), which in Swift's parody produces only a temporary physical purification and no discernible amelioration of the moral imperfections of its human figures—such as the sempstress, the spruce Templer, the "dagged Females" who "Pretend to cheapen Goods," and the normally contentious Whigs and Tories who gather under one roof to "save their Wigs" (ll. 33-42). Hints of the biblical Deluge appear in the opening lines of the second of the poem's four divisions, which echo Milton's description of Noah's Flood in *Paradise Lost*:

> MEAN while the South rising with dabbled Wings,
> A Sable Cloud a-thwart the Welkin flings,
> That swill'd more Liquor than it could contain,
> And like a Drunkard gives it up again.[5]
>
> (ll. 13-16)

"Flood" is the last word of the poem (l. 63). To the biblical implications of the all-inclusive overflow of sewage and garbage in the fourth section (ll. 53-63), the opening lines of the third section add further classical notions of a cleansing catastrophe, such as the burning of Troy and—mockingly—something equivalent to the establishment of a new and better Troy in Latium: "Now in contiguous Drops the Flood comes down,/Threat'ning with Deluge this *Devoted* Town" (ll. 31-32).[6] The futility of expecting any improvement through this transformation is suggested in the same section by Swift's comparison of an eighteenth-century London beau, quaking in his sedan chair, to the "Bully *Greeks*" who fear their ruse of the "Trojan horse" will be exposed by Laocoön's spear (ll. 43-52).

In matters of eschatology, Swift's fascination with Ovidian metamorphoses or Christian miracles that produce little, if any, change or improvement can be seen in "Verses on the Death of Dr. Swift." Here, the "resurrection" in the concluding panegyric, no matter how stirring and true we find it in the main, is shot through with shameless distortions and even outright falsifications of fact.[7] This "resurrection" resembles a moth emerging from its chrysalis, a conventional analogue that actually occurs in "Vanbrug's House" to describe the "rebirth" of a building in a smaller size (ll. 29-54). In "The Day of Judgement," the ultimate collective transfiguration proves unworkable because the human race lacks the moral stature needed for damnation in the traditional Christian sense.

Among Swift's poems depicting ineffectual metamorphoses or miracles in mid-life situations, the two most prominent are "Baucis and Philemon" (which survives in two versions) and "Vanbrug's House" (surviving in three). In the latter poem the house Sir John constructs for himself from the ruins of Whitehall Palace (which had been destroyed by fire in 1703) comes out much diminished from the original, like a phoenix arising from its ashes a fraction of its former size (ll. 121-22). Significantly, in "Vanbrug's House," as in a number of Swift's other poems, the mock-metamorphosis employs one or more metaphors or analogues whose validity or even plausibility the reader may at first be inclined to challenge. Thus an equivalence is imaginatively assumed among Vanbrugh's three principal activities: play-writing, architecture (he designed Blenheim Palace), and heraldry. As herald, architect, and playwright, "he can in a Day/Repair a *House* gone to Decay" (ll. 37-38), with a pun on "house" as lineage, a building, or the management of a playhouse. Adapting the legend of Amphion, Swift claims, tongue in cheek, that Vanbrugh can use his skill as a playwright to erect an equivalent physical structure:

> *THE Building, as the Poet Writ,*
> *Rose in proportion to his Wit:*
> *And first the Prologue built a Wall*
> *So wide as to encompass all.*
> *The Scene, a Wood, produc'd no more*

> *Than a few Scrubby Trees before.*
> *The Plot as yet lay deep, and so*
> *A Cellar next was dug below:*
> *But this a Work so hard was found,*
> *Two Acts it cost him under Ground.*
> *Two other Acts we may presume*
> *Were spent in Building each a Room;*
> *Thus far advanc't, he made a shift*
> *To raise a Roof with Act the Fift.*
> *The Epilogue behind, did frame*
> *A Place not decent here to name.*
>
> (ll. 79-94)

Typically, the humor involved in progressively widening the gap between the tenor and vehicle of the metaphor leaves the reader torn between skepticism and amusement. One may, indeed, feel uncertain which is the tenor and which is the vehicle.[8]

A more broadly meaningful mid-life metamorphosis occurs to the old couple in "The Story of Baucis and Philemon." Here, the tenor or vehicle of the metaphor (it is difficult to know which is which) consists of Ovid's story as translated by Dryden and published in Dryden's highly popular volume of *Fables* (1700) only a half-dozen years before Swift wrote the earlier version of his poem. The Ovidian transformation and the Christian miracle become, in Swift's mocking metamorphoses, a depiction of Baucis and Philemon as "twice-born" Christians who were more truly religious *before* they were "born again."[9] In Swift's list of household appurtenances that get changed into furnishings for the parish church, some come off slightly better, some slightly worse, some neither better nor worse:

> Scarce had they spoke when fair and soft
> The Roof began to mount aloft
> Aloft rose ev'ry Beam and Rafter,
> The heavy Wall went clamb'ring after.
> The Chimny widen'd and grew high'r,

Became a Steeple with a Spire:
The Kettle to the Top was hoist
And there stood fastned to a Joyst,
But with the upside doun to shew
It's Inclination for below; . . .
The groaning Chair began to crawll
Like a huge Insect up the Wall,
There stuck, and to a Pulpitt grew,
But kept it's Matter and it's Hue,
And mindfull of it's antient State,
Still Groans while tatling Gossips prate.
(ll. 91-100, 105-10)

Baucis and Philemon themselves, however, are less truly pious in their new, more exalted, "twice-born" state than they were previously. The description of Philemon as a parson typifies what happens to both husband and wife:

He spoke, and presently he feels
His Grazier's Coat reach down his Heels,
The Sleeves new border'd with a List
Widn'd and gatherd at his Wrist;
But being old continued just
As threadbare, and as full of Dust.
A shambling awkward Gate he took,
With a demure dejected Look.
Talkt of his Off'rings, Tyths, and Dues,
Could Smoak, and Drink, and read the News;
Or sell a Goose at the next Toun
Decently hid beneath his Goun.
(ll. 165-76)

Even before they are "twice-born," the sincerity of the pair is questioned by their being called "Goodman Philemon" and "Goody Baucis" and by the repeated labeling of their heavenly visitors as Puritan "Saints."[10]

"The Story of Baucis and Philemon" uses metaphor implicitly to describe a metamorphosis that changes nothing essential. In "The Description of a Salamander," Swift goes to the opposite extreme by employing a blatantly overt metaphor to transform its subject—in this case, Lord Cutts, the distinguished military commander—into something almost beyond recognition. As vehicle replaces tenor, the reader finds himself committed to all sorts of qualities in the tenor—that is, Lord Cutts—that he might otherwise resist. Vehicle and tenor diverge from one another to the point where, in this classic instance of "open" form, the gap between them becomes unbridgeable, and the reader must give preference to vehicle over tenor. Starting with Pliny's description of a salamander as "something that will conquer fire," as Cutts conquered cannon fire in battle, Swift relentlessly develops his point-by-point comparison:

> FIRST then, our Author has defin'd
> This Reptil, of the Serpent kind,
> With gawdy Coat, and shining Train,
> But loathsom Spots his Body stain:
> Out from some Hole obscure he flies
> When Rains descend, and Tempests rise,
> Till the Sun clears the Air; and then
> Crawls back neglected to his Den.
> (ll. 29-36)

Similar in technique to "The Description of a Salamander" is "The Fable of Midas," in which the subject is the Duke of Marlborough, with his alleged avarice, while the vehicle of the metaphor is Ovid's well-known fable. One difference, however, is that the vehicle that metamorphoses Marlborough into Midas is itself a story of metamorphoses:

> *MIDAS,* we are in Story told
> Turn'd ev'ry thing he touch't to *Gold:*
> He *chip't* his *Bread,* the Pieces round
> Glitter'd like Spangles on the Ground:
> A Codling e'er it went his Lip in,
> Would strait become a *Golden* Pippin:

He call'd for Drink, you saw him Sup
Potable Gold in *Golden Cup.*
His empty Paunch that he might fill,
He suck't his Vittels thro' a Quill;
Untouch't it pass't between his Grinders,
Or't had been happy for *Gold-finders.*
He cock't his Hat, you would have said
Mambrino's Helm adorn'd his Head.

(ll. 1-14)

He could turn *"Dung* it self to *Gold"* (l. 48). As Swift's comparison continues, even the transformation of Midas's ears into those of an ass is exploited, for Marlborough is implicitly accused of being insensitive to the claims of literary patronage. The poem concludes: "And *Midas* now neglected stands, / With *Asses Ears,* and *dirty Hands"* (ll. 81-82).

Similar also to the poems on Cutts and Marlborough is "The Virtues of Sid Hamet the Magician's Rod," which satirizes Sidney Godolphin. Besides the multiple comparisons it draws between Godolphin's white staff of office and other rods, the transforming metaphor of this poem includes an allusion to Cid Hamete Benengeli, the fictitious Arab author of *Don Quixote,* and of course there is the pervasive phallic connotation of the rod. An important difference from the two other poems is that in "The Virtues of Sid Hamet" the sequence of metaphors is discontinuous, since Godolphin's staff is compared to a variety of rods. Also, whereas Godolphin's rod is sometimes analogous to these other rods, elsewhere it produces just the opposite effect. Thus, although the wand of Moses was "harmless" while he

held it in his Hand,
But soon as e'er he *lay'd it down,*
'Twas a devouring Serpent grown[,]
OUR great Magician, *Hamet Sid,*
Reverses what the Prophet did;
His *Rod* was honest *English* Wood,

> That, senseless, in a Corner stood,
> Till Metamorphos'd by his Grasp,
> It grew an all-devouring Asp.
>
> (ll. 1-10)

Godolphin's staff is compared to a witch's broomstick, a divining rod, the rod of Hermes, a fishing pole, a conjurer's rod, Achilles' scepter, and so forth. Unlike the conjurer's rod, which keeps *"mischievous Spirits* out," Godolphin's is designed "to *take them in*" (ll. 52, 56). Unlike Achilles' staff, which was "a sapless Twig,"

> *Sid*'s Scepter, full of Juice, did shoot
> In Golden Boughs, and Golden Fruit,
> And He, the *Dragon* never sleeping,
> Guarded each fair *Hesperian* Pippin.
>
> (ll. 71-74)

More complex than the three lampoons on Cutts, Marlborough, and Godolphin is Swift's relatively late "metaphor" poem, "The Progress of Beauty," written in 1719. In this poem the tenor and the vehicle of the metaphor derive from the conventional comparison of a woman, here represented by a hypothetical "Celia," to the moon, or Diana. Vehicle is immediately substituted for tenor, however, and each metamorphoses the other as the moon is initially described in terms more appropriate to Celia, whose defects are less visible at a distance than they are close by:

> When first Diana leaves her Bed
> Vapors and Steams her Looks disgrace,
> A frouzy dirty colour'd red
> Sits on her cloudy wrinckled Face.
>   But by degrees when mounted high
> Her artificiall Face appears
> Down from her Window in the Sky,
> Her Spots are gone, her Visage clears.
>   'Twixt earthly Femals and the Moon

All Parallells exactly run;
If Celia should appear too soon
Alas, the Nymph would be undone.

(ll. 1-12)

Swift's point-by-point comparison of woman and moon concludes by emphasizing how changeable they are, with the monthly waning of the moon representing the transience of woman's beauty.

It is remarkable that so many of the poems Swift wrote after his early odes and before the resurgence of his personal, poetical, and political activities in Ireland around 1719 can be understood as transforming metaphors or metaphorical metamorphoses. The earliest such poem, "Verses wrote in a Lady's *Ivory Table-Book,* Anno 1698," metaphorically equates table-book and lady in its opening couplet: "Peruse my Leaves thro' ev'ry Part, / And think thou seest my owners Heart" (ll. 1-2). As the poem spills forth its artful inventory of the clutter in the lady's heart and in her book, anyone writing in the book, including the speaker of the poem, who paradoxically writes this poem in the book to warn people *against* writing anything there, is metamorphosed into a phallic "Tool" (l. 28), fittest "in all Points" (l. 28), "a Gold Pencil tipt with Lead" (l. 30).[11] The elegy on Partridge, who was metamorphosed from life to death "on the 29th of this Instant *March,* 1708," turns on an "Analogy . . . 'twixt *Cobling* and *Astrology.*" This particular metamorphosis changes nothing, for those who did their "Fortunes seek" (l. 109) from the charlatan Partridge when he was still alive will find that his grave

> has so much *Virtue in't,*
> *That I durst Pawn my Ears, 'twill tell*
> *Whate'er concerns you full as well,*
> *In* Physick, Stolen Goods, *or* Love,
> *As he himself could, when above.*

(ll. 112-16)

In "Apollo Outwitted," a metamorphosis similar to the one in the implied metaphorical comparison to the story of Daphne is thwarted because Ardelia—better known to us as the poetess Anne Finch, Countess of Winchilsea—already knows the story:

> OVID had warn'd her to beware,
>   Of Stroling God's, whose usual Trade is,
> Under pretense of Taking Air,
>   To pick up Sublunary Ladies.
>
>   (ll. 21-24)

The climax of Swift's metaphor/metamorphosis poems is surely "Cadenus and Vanessa," which he composed in 1713. In this poem, the longest he ever wrote, Swift used a multiplicity of metaphorical "frames," in the sense popularized by Erving Goffman,[12] in a vain attempt to cool off Esther Vanhomrigh's torrid infatuation for him—attempted, in other words, to use art to metamorphose real life, to "make things happen." Any list of the "frames" or metaphorical contexts Swift employed must be open-ended and perhaps endless. There are the classical gods and goddesses; the legal proceedings; the Court-of-Love format and other pastoral-courtly-romance contexts; the fashionable London social scene in 1713; traditional forms of comedy including farce, humor, satire, and irony; even the fictitious names "Cadenus" and "Vanessa"; and, among many other things, the question of man's (or woman's) relationship to the justice of "Heaven." Swift's attempt was unsuccessful, as we know, since Esther Vanhomrigh pursued him to Dublin in 1714 and may have posthumously embarrassed him, after her death there in 1723, by prearranging the publication of this very poem three years later, in 1726. The poem boomeranged with a vengeance.

"Cadenus and Vanessa," then, was an unsuccessful attempt to use art to metamorphose life. In this same poem, however, as we are just beginning to appreciate fully, Swift's dazzling array of metaphors transforms the raw material of life into high art. Such is the case with all great poems: life is the tenor of the metaphor and the poem itself the vehicle, which miraculously metamorphoses life into something more harmonious, whole, and radiant. Viewed this way, Swift the poet is no different from, and not less great than, his contemporaries Pope and Dryden.

NOTES

1. See John Irwin Fischer, *On Swift's Poetry* (Gainesville: University Presses of Florida, 1978), especially pp. 72-95. "Swift," remarks Fischer, "becomes, in Rothstein's fine phrase, 'the master of metamorphosis' " (p. 74).

2. The first three of these four poems are discussed, along with "A Serious Poem upon William Wood" (1724), by A. B. England, "The Subversion of Logic in Some Poems by Swift," *Studies in English Literature* 15 (1975): 409-18. Metaphor/metamorphosis poems were, of course, written by Swift outside my limiting dates of 1698-1719, but they are less centrally important.

3. See also my *"Fiat Lux:* Logos versus Chaos in Swift's 'A Description of the Morning,' " *Papers on Language and Literature* 8 (1972): 302-7. This article cites all important earlier discussions of the poem.

4. All quotations of Swift's poetry are from *The Poems of Jonathan Swift,* ed. Sir Harold Williams, 3 vols., 2d ed. (Oxford: Clarendon Press, 1958).

5. *Paradise Lost,* 11: 738-40; see Fischer, pp. 95-109, for a selected list of earlier discussions of the "Shower."

6. As usual in this period, *"Devoted"* is a Latinism meaning both "sacred to the gods" and "doomed to destruction." Cf. Swift's "The Author upon Himself" (ll. 59-60): "Now, through the Realm a Proclamation spread,/ To fix a Price on his *devoted* Head" (emphasis added).

7. See my essay "The Mystery of Personal Identity: Swift's Verses on His Own Death," in *The Author in His Work: Essays on a Problem in Criticism,* ed. Louis L. Martz and Aubrey Williams (New Haven, Conn.: Yale University Press, 1978), pp. 245-62.

8. See also "On the Little House by the Church Yard of Castleknock," especially ll. 1-12.

9. For this suggestion, as well as for several others in my essay, I am indebted to an unpublished paper by my former student Brittain A. Blair, "Metaparody in Swift's Early Poetry."

10. See also ll. 52, 56, and passim. For the passage on Baucis, see ll. 137-44. Rebecca Price Parkin treats Swift's anti-Puritan satire in "Swift's *Baucis and Philemon:* A Sermon in the Burlesque Mode," *Satire Newsletter* 7 (1970): 109-14.

5

Rhetorical Order and Emotional Turbulence in "Cadenus and Vanessa"

A. B. ENGLAND

University of Victoria

In a great deal of Augustan poetry there is a contrast between highly ordered rhetorical systems and the disorderly subject matter that those systems define. In most instances the effect of this contrast is to diminish the subject matter by making it seem to fall woefully short of the authoritative order embodied by the poem's rhetoric. In Swift's poems, however, rhetorical systems marked by an obtrusive degree of orderliness often appear to be subverted or challenged by those elements within the poetry which are in contrast with them. "Cadenus and Vanessa" is an example of one way in which this happens. Although there is a noticeable and persistent rhetorical ordering of the central experience, Swift constantly implies the presence in that experience of unruly forces that are not adequately contained by the several frameworks imposed on them.

The opening debate about love's decline, which gives rise to the action of the poem, takes the form of a lawsuit and is thus structured according to the terms of a systematic and traditional device of social organization. But there is a comic contrast in the first pleader's speech between the emotionally charged issue at its center and the formal phraseology of the law courts.[1] One critic points out that this phraseology represents an attempt "to reduce the wild question of love to reasonable proportions—to render it orderly, manageable and discussable by circumscribing it with precedents . . . and the rhetoric of logic."[2] Swift's use of legal terms in this context is an early instance of his adopting verbal patterns that systematize and stylize the treatment of an emotionally complex issue, and there is an immediate discrepancy between this particular process of stylization and the subject upon which it is brought to bear.

Since the debate over love's decline is cast in the form of a trial, its participants require a clear-cut verdict in which blame will be allocated to one of the two sides. After the first pleader has blamed the men, the "Defendant's Council" seeks to exculpate them by blaming the nature of women. His speech contains a rigid argument in which two absolute concepts are juxtaposed so as to lead toward a definitive conclusion. First, he describes the love that was celebrated by the "antient Poets" as "A Fire celestial, chaste, refin'd, / Conceiv'd and kindled in the Mind." Then he argues that such love no longer exists because "Women now feel no such Fire, / And only know the gross Desire"; love has thus degenerated into lust because the emotions of women are now capable of moving only in "lower Spheres." All this leads to a rather clear verdict, introduced by an emphatic "Hence we conclude," and enforced by a diagrammatic sequence of oppositions in which "Fools, Fops, and Rakes" are juxtaposed with "Virtue, Wit, and Parts" (ll. 23-66). The second pleader's response to the problem, then, is to construct a noticeably ordered rhetorical pattern that reduces the issues to a definitive clarity; but his speech does not succeed in resolving the matter for

Venus, who remains in a state of uncertainty. Indeed, as the poem progresses, it persistently suggests that the type of verbal structure on which the pleader rests his case is inadequate to deal with the problem it is designed to resolve.

Venus subsequently seeks a course of action that will both resolve the issues into the form of a decisive verdict and reestablish her reputation among the gods. She conceives the "Project" (l. 132) of transforming a newly born girl into a paragon of excellence in order that the men will no longer be able to complain that womankind cannot provide worthy objects of love. In thus seeking to construct an answer to the second pleader's arguments, she does not question the absolutist and categorizing tendencies of his speech. She too seeks to allocate blame decisively on one side or the other; if Vanessa succeeds in raising a "Flame that will endure/ For ever, uncorrupt and pure" (ll. 144-45), then it will be proved that the women have been to blame for the absence of such love prior to Vanessa's appearance, and if she does not succeed, it will be proved that the men have been at fault. Venus sets about implementing her project in a very systematic fashion. She will probe into every area of human activity so as to "gather" the virtues that she requires, and then she is going to "unite" them into a personality that will be both inclusive and harmonious (ll. 148-53). Venus proceeds to graft onto the beauty Vanessa already possesses such traditional female qualities as "Sweetness" (l. 161), "Decency of Mind" (l. 164), and a "soft, engaging Air" (l. 178). Then she tricks Pallas into providing a series of "manly" virtues such as "Knowledge," "Judgment," "Wit," "Fortitude," and "Honour" (ll. 202-9). Vanessa's personality is thus formed by a methodical process of selection and organization, and Venus responds to the initial problem by creating a highly structured artifact that is designed both to resolve her uncertainty and to render her position secure. Since this fictionalized creation of Vanessa is intended by Swift as a comment on the actual personality of Esther Vanhomrigh, it also constitutes an engagement by the author himself in a creative act that erects a systematized and stylized version of a human personality. But although he describes Vanessa at this point by means of a noticeably ordered verbal pattern, the experience that Swift eventually dramatizes is in radical contrast with the order embodied by such a process of definition, and he soon indicates that Venus's plan to establish Vanessa as a didactic model for womankind is doomed to failure (l. 249).

When Vanessa at last makes her entry into the real world of men and women, she confronts a crowd of "fashionable Fops" whose conversation is an utter chaos of trivial and disconnected items (ll. 318-27). After responding with "silent Scorn," she seeks to test their "Wisdom" by means of a speech that in some ways resembles that of the second pleader in the trial (ll. 334-55). In communicating her vision of life to the fops, she insists on certain clear-cut evaluative distinctions, and she uses carefully balanced rhetorical patterns to enforce them; "Titles, Figure, Shape, and Dress," for instance, are systematically opposed to "Judgment, Knowledge, Wit, and Taste," and the moral character of "present Times" is weighed in the balance with that of "*Greeks* and *Romans.*" This formal set-piece appears to emanate from a mind that is confident of its ability to arrange and dispose the materials at its command. But especially when Vanessa names and describes the "antient Heroes" and talks of "foreign Customs," it becomes clear that the speech constitutes a withdrawal from the world she is confronting toward materials that are almost exclusively drawn from her reading, materials that she can arrange into such a systematic pattern. Vanessa responds to the chaos she encounters by constructing a self-contained and ordered artifact that separates her from this chaos.

It soon becomes clear that Vanessa's behavior is not bringing about the consequences that Venus had in mind when she created her. She withdraws from and alienates the majority of the people with whom she comes into contact, and her relationship with the exclusive circle over which she presides is not evidently conducive to the emergence of sexual passion. Observing this situation, Cupid now prepares to intervene and to take "Vengeance" for what he regards as his mother's "Wrongs" (ll. 466-71). Angry and "full of Mischief," he is clearly conceived at this point in his traditional role as an agent of disorder, and he is bent on destroying the highly structured world that Vanessa has created for herself.

Swift's rendering of the moment at which Cupid makes her fall in love with Cadenus indicates his procedure in the rest of the poem (ll. 510-23). He describes the sudden emergence of sexual passion in Vanessa, but the terms of the narrative at this point involve a particularly high degree of formalizing and distancing stylization. First, Swift uses a mythological framework by which Vanessa's emotions are described in the traditional terms of Cupid and his arrows. Then he reports that one of these arrows both penetrated and was made more effective by a volume of Cadenus's "Poetic Works." This elegant narrative device provides Swift's rendering of the moment with a further degree of stylized patterning. The fact that no such volume as Swift's "Poetic Works" existed when he wrote "Cadenus and Vanessa" only increases our awareness of the distance between actual experience and the fictional structures that Swift invents. The passage manages, however, to suggest that some very strong emotions are at work. When Swift stresses that Cupid shoots this particular arrow "with all his Strength," he reveals the accumulated anger and frustration that are involved in his attitude toward Vanessa. When he refers to the "Pains unknown" and the "Smart" that the piercing of Vanessa's breast creates, he implies that her experience is one of considerable intensity. Thus, although the passage manifests a tendency toward an elegant and distancing process of fictionalization, it also makes it clear that Vanessa is being affected by powerful emotional forces.

Once these forces take possession of Vanessa, Cadenus becomes unable to understand her behavior. He has been able to define his relationship with her by reference to certain clear-cut categories and structures—they have been like a "Father" and a "Child," or like a "Master" and "the finest Boy" (ll. 548-53)—but a "sudden Change" occurs, and instead of attending to his lessons she allows her mind to "range" wildly in a manner that Cadenus can neither predict nor understand (ll. 560-67). His initial response to the change is to try to define it by means of a traditional category: "And first he modestly conjectures/His Pupil might be tir'd with Lectures" (ll. 568-69). This is an attempt by Cadenus to rationalize the disorder he confronts by explaining it in terms of a familiar syndrome. We already know, of course, that it is not an adequate explanation, and the element of comedy in the rhyme appears calculated to make it sound slightly absurd. But this analysis provides Cadenus with an ordering, definitive framework within which to place the new behavior pattern and thus to render it more manageable than it might otherwise be. He says that he has engaged in an educational "Project" that he discovers is too "dull" and enclosing for her, and that it has failed because it did not adequately take "Nature" into account (ll. 575-87). Cadenus is thus enabled to reach a conclusion that is not acutely disturbing because it involves reference to certain familiar behavioral landmarks that the teacher has learned to accept. The reader, however, is aware that although his emphasis on "Nature" is indeed relevant to Vanessa's experience, it is relevant in a much more disturbing way than Cadenus understands.

Although Vanessa feels an impulse toward "Tears" on hearing Cadenus's analysis, she has been taught the importance of self-control and "Dignity" (l. 595), and in her declaration of love she attempts to form a rationalistic defense of the passion that Cadenus has aroused. First she invokes two "Maxims" that he has taught her: that "Virtue . . . knows nothing which it dare not own" and that "common Forms were not design'd/Directors to a noble Mind." Then she argues that although Cadenus has warned her about the "Charms" possessed by "Men of Wit," he has not provided her with the equipment to resist them. And she concludes that his "Lessons found the weakest Part,/Aim'd at the Head, but reach'd the Heart" (ll. 606-23). Vanessa thus employs Cadenus's own teachings so as to build an argument that both defines and justifies an intense emotion. But the fact that she constructs her speech as a deliberate effort to maintain her "Dignity" in the face of disrupting forces suggests that she is aware of a discrepancy between the order embodied by that speech and the experience it purports to define. Moreover, since her argument refers so consistently to Cadenus's teachings, it creates the impression that she is trying to provide him with the type of analysis that will enable him to accept her love.

The above speech is designed to enforce the conclusion that Cadenus has aroused an emotional rather than a rational response (his lessons reached her "Heart"). But Vanessa is soon forced by his embarrassed reaction to adopt a different tactic; she argues that since her own virtues have become identifiable with those of her teacher, she is acting in accord with the principle of self-love, and that she has been directed into this state by a rational admiration of the virtues Cadenus embodies (ll. 674-87). The discrepancy between this argument and her earlier one is enough to suggest that Vanessa's speech involves a degree of insincere manipulation on her part and a degree of irony on the part of the author. The final couplet—"Why she likes him, admire not at her,/She loves herself, and that's the Matter"—almost reduces her argument to the level of farce. This is the second occasion on which Swift has introduced a comic rhyme at a point where a speaker is engaged in the rationalistic analysis of passionate behavior, and the effect is again to lightly undercut the speaker's procedure. In this instance the undercutting is a device by which Swift suggests not only that Vanessa's rationalizations are inadequate to define the experience to which they allude, but also that they may not be completely sincere. She may discuss her love for Cadenus as if she were engaged in a formal debate, but the primary impulse toward the structures of such debate appears to come from Cadenus. There is also this crucial difference between them: whereas Cadenus obviously wants to believe that such structures bear a natural and direct correlation with the experience they are both confronting, Vanessa knows from the onset of her emotion that they do not.

Swift, as author, is engaged in a structuring and rationalizing process, too, in that he transposes a difficult personal experience into the patterns of orderly debate. When he describes Vanessa's "Eloquence" in disputing this new "Topick" (ll. 714-15), he uses the debate analogy in such a way as to place the conversation in a familiar conceptual framework that plays down the unsettling aspects of the experience. But when he goes on to stress the element of "Passion" that inspires Vanessa to eloquence, it becomes clear that the framework provided by the analogy is being introduced ironically, in full recognition of the distance between its comforting intimations of order and the nature of the experience to which it is applied.

Eventually Cadenus becomes unable to "oppose *Vanessa's* Flame" and is forced to accept the reality of her passion, but the situation is so baffling for him that he still clings to a reassuring framework by thinking of himself as a figure defeated in a debate by one whose arguments have been conducted with extraordinary eloquence (ll. 744-49). When he experiences a sensation of "Pride" in being loved by Vanessa (ll. 750-51), he again attempts to rationalize both her behavior and his own feelings by attributing the growth of her passion to an appreciative "Judgment" of his "Merit." In the couplet that concludes these ruminations—"She noted all she ever read,/And had a most discerning Head" (ll. 756-57)— Swift quite openly ridicules Cadenus's terms of reference and makes it clear that the terminology of the classroom is absurdly inappropriate to the experience it purports to describe. Cadenus's tendency to erect ordering and reassuring systems of analysis in response to the emotions he confronts appears to manifest itself once again when he proposes an alternative to the kind of passion that Vanessa both feels in herself and wants to arouse in him. In the passage defining a "Friendship" based on "rational" esteem there is a close correlation between the order of the rhetoric and the nature of the relationship being offered (ll. 780-89). Actually, the speech constitutes another of those verbal systems by which Cadenus persistently seeks to evade Vanessa's passion. Since its terms are discordant with her emotional state, she can only reject them and embark upon her attempt to break down his resistance to those intensities of feeling which have become so central to her own experience.

At this point Swift leaves the major characters in a state of impasse and reintroduces Venus, who has observed the consequences of her project and appears to have reached a decisive conclusion. She claims that she is ready to "decide" the issues of the original debate (l. 837), and she goes on to pronounce a verdict "against the *Men*" (l. 853) for having been so undiscriminating as not to fall in love with Vanessa. Venus has thus apparently emerged from her earlier state of uncertainty and has been enabled to reach the verdict that initially eluded her. But the speech in which she announces this verdict is characterized by a strident, frustrated tone, and it contains much emotional falsifying of the issues. She complains "grievously" that she has been "cheated" by the men, that she went to "Lord knows what Expense" to create

6

Faith, Hope, and Charity in Swift's Poems to Stella

JOHN IRWIN FISCHER

Louisiana State University

Meditating on Swift's relationship with Esther Johnson and on the poems that testify to that relationship and partly shaped it, several critics have remarked that neither the poems nor the relationship exhibit much evidence of Christian sensibilities.[1] Nevertheless, the most knotty passages in Swift's poems to Stella gain in coherence and power when they are examined within the context of Christian thought about faith, hope, and charity. Thus, if the best reading of a poem is the fullest possible reading consonant with the poem's explicit doctrine, then Swift's poems to Stella are best read as Christian verse.

Swift wrote all his poems to Stella late in her life. Of course, "late in life" is a relative term; in 1719, when Swift addressed his first birthday poem to her, Stella was only thirty-eight. But she died less than nine years later, in 1728, and at a time near her death Swift remarked that he "long knew that [his] dear Friend had not the *Stamina Vitae*."[2]

Because Swift knew this, his poems to Stella reflect both his awareness of her continuing decay and his anxiety lest she veer toward despair. Generically, his poems are consolations; they are comic and imaginative attempts to reconcile Stella to mortality.

The imaginative quality of the Stella poems is best demonstrated by placing them within a recognizable tradition of consolatory philosophy. Given the shape of Western thought, there are three basic choices: epicurean (clearly not a Swiftian choice), stoic, or one of several possible Christian traditions.[3] Most readers have argued that the Stella poems are stoic in character: attempts to reconcile Stella to the misfortunes of everyday mortality by exhibiting for her the delight she might properly take in her own virtuous fortitude.[4] This argument is partially correct, for Swift repeatedly tells Stella that virtue is its own reward and that this reward is sufficient. Further, not only do Swift's poems reiterate this traditionally stoic response to common mortality, they exhibit other characteristic elements of stoic thought as well. When in "To Stella, Who Collected and Transcribed his Poems" Swift observes that poets safely can praise human virtue, but not human beauty, because beauty is "what Stoicks call *without our Power*"[5] (l. 63), he reveals the importance of Stoicism to these poems.

Nevertheless, though stoic elements occur consistently in the poems to Stella, the poems themselves are not finally stoic in character; Stella herself tells us why not. In her single birthday poem to Swift she describes what she thought Swift had taught her. "You taught how I might youth prolong," she begins surprisingly,

> By Knowing what was right and wrong;
> How from my heart to bring supplies
> Of lustre to my fading eyes;
> How soon a beauteous mind repairs
> The loss of chang'd or falling hairs;

> How wit and virtue from within
> Send out a smoothness o'er the skin.
> ("To Dr. Swift on his birth-day," ll.
>   33-40)

This synopsis of Swift's lore is not essentially stoic, but Christian. Stella's insistence that a sound heart and mind are lifelong goods while the flesh continuously decays is stoic. But her related claims that moral wisdom prolongs youth, a good heart brightens faded eyes, and wit and virtue smooth an aging face assert that flesh itself can ultimately be transfigured by the spirit. Apparently, Stella found this assertion central to the wisdom Swift taught her. In Western cultures, this assertion is Christian.

To parallel Stella's remarks with Christian belief is not to claim that the Stella poems simply exhibit Christian doctrine. But the parallel does suggest the usefulness of reviewing a few doctrinal matters.[6] For the Christian the distinction that stoic authors traditionally draw between body and spirit is only an effect of pride. The stoic wishes to distinguish between what is within his power and what is not; thus he struggles to perfect his spirit but accepts the decay of flesh with resignation. On the other hand, the Christian believes that both his spirit and his flesh degenerated because of the Fall. Without God's grace no man can conduct himself well, and everyone is damned; but the agency of grace operates so that all men can live well within the promised resurrection of both body and spirit. Life defines itself for the Christian (whose most vital symbols mix flesh and spirit) not as a struggle to free spirit from flesh, but rather as a drama in which each man seeks, in grace, to harmonize his flesh and spirit with each other and with God's super-intending will.

Swift's intention in all the Stella poems is to teach his friend how to integrate herself within this Christian drama. In order to examine how Swift went about his task, it is necessary to note a final point about Christian reality. Unlike stoicism, which argues that men can achieve a proud indifference to the whole of an objective world, Christianity maintains that no man can escape what really is. That is why, for example, if a Christian is comforted by his faith as he faces death, he must assume that his comfort reflects a real state of affairs and is not simply an achieved consolation. For the Christian there is no objective world beyond the world that faith presents to him. Rather, the objective world of number, weight, and measure is for the Christian only a nightmare from which he has been awakened by faith. This distinction is most important for the Stella poems, because in them Swift's first effort is to preserve Stella from the nightmare of death-in-matter.

Swift performs this task very skillfully; indeed, he effects Stella's enlightenment with such grace and wit that he often obscures for us what he accomplished for her. For example, generations of critics have remarked that Swift was in error as he began his first birthday poem to Stella; she was thirty-eight at the time it was written, but it begins with the statement, "Stella this Day is thirty four." Despite the inaccuracy of this line, there is no reason to think that Swift did not know Stella's true age as he wrote it. His next line reads, "We won't dispute a Year or more," and thus tacitly acknowledges that Stella is thirty-four only by courtesy. The real importance of Swift's line, then, is not that it represents an instance of Swift's faulty memory, but rather that it records his refusal to count the clock that tells the time. The line insists that, for Swift, even the verities of simple arithmetic are subject to sudden and surprising revisions; impressively, Swift makes this boast good in the rest of his poem by demonstrating his ability to transform even time's grimmest effects into delight and instruction. Working in puns, false quantities, half truths, and whole lies, Swift shows Stella the ways to make light of her weightiest infirmities. He achieves something of the status of that god who, at the close of the poem, creates two young and beautiful nymphs out of Stella's multiplied years and bulky size; like that god he shows himself able to make much of value from his friend's troublesome superfluities.

Of course, it may seem naive to credit with sober meaning Swift's comic manipulations in "On Stella's Birth-day, 1718/19." Happily, though, in "To Stella, Who Collected and Transcribed his Poems" Swift himself takes up the problem of truth in verse. Nothing except a full-scale reading can really illuminate this richly layered poem, but even a cursory inspection suggests two important points. First, insofar as the poem's artful ambiguities can be reduced to didactic statement about poetry and truth at all, the statement the poem makes is this: poets can find their truths neither in abstract ideas (such ideas quickly become hackneyed) nor in matter itself (because matter is in perpetual flux); therefore, poets must make their truths by informing matter with ideas and bracing ideas with matter in such a way (to use Swift's brilliant phrase) as to "insinuate what is true" (l. 60). Obviously, this is a very radical vision of the poet's function, but this function exactly describes the task Swift set himself in "To Stella, Who Collected and Transcribed his Poems": to tell Stella, who habitually rejected all criticism, that her habitual conduct is itself faulty. In order to convince Stella of her fault, Swift must first neutralize her habitual rejection of criticism, and that is impossible unless she first recognizes her fault. Thus, Swift sets a conundrum in this poem that can be escaped only by assuming, with him, that the poet works between what is and what should be to make the truth he cannot find.

To make this assumption is to teeter frighteningly near complete subjectivity. But, as Swift knew, everyone teeters there most of the time anyway. Whenever we know anything, our knowing is simply an event and not a fact. Of course, we can choose to "believe in" such events; for example, we can suppose that the things we see are "really there." But when we make this supposition, we do so only on trust; for there is utterly no way to prove that the process by which we seem to bring together an apparent self with an apparent world has any ontological reality at all.

In the outrageous lines that conclude "Stella's Birth-Day, 1724/25" Swift drives home this truth. Claiming that Stella has not grown old, and basing his claim on the evidence of his "dimmish" vision, he defies us to refute him. In truth, we cannot. We can say that our vision is sharper than his, but he does not deny that. We cannot say that our vision is "more true" than his, for our claim to trust our senses for truth is neither better nor worse than his claim to trust his. That is why, when he tells Stella that "Nature, always in the Right/ To your Decays adapts my Sight" (ll. 43-44), we can only concur; to do anything else must call our own sight into question.

In effect, then, in the Stella poems Swift literally dissolves for us, as well as for Stella, the whole world of hard facts and unworkable matter, and in its place he substitutes a world in which anything is true that can fairly be seen to be true. Ultimately, Swift does not want to deny the truth of Stella's aging, or her growing decrepitude, or her imminent death, for he can see these alterations well enough in spite of his dimmish eyes. But Swift does want to affirm that even these alterations can be truly good if one has faith enough to make them so.

The chief end of all the poems Swift wrote for Stella is to inculcate such faith in her. His strategies to effect this end vary from poem to poem. In "Stella's Birth-Day, 1718/19" he demonstrates that neither Stella's years nor her girth are such solid antagonists that they cannot be reformed into jest and instruction. In "Stella's Birth-Day: A great Bottle of Wine, long buried, being that Day dug up" he comically exhibits how even a fit of poetic dryness can be distilled and exalted into poetry. And in "To Stella, Visiting me in my Sickness" he reminds Stella how she herself reformed his own sickened vision more than once by teaching him to bless what before he only cursed. Different as these three poems are, they all share one common end; like every poem Swift wrote for her, they encourage Stella to recognize and trust that the world she had come to regard as alien and hostile was full of creative possibilities if she willed it to be so.

But not all the poems to Stella equally exhibit Swift's faith and the creative powers that flowed therefrom. To see the world as rich with meaning requires a continuous receptivity to it, and in one way Swift's receptivity was always astonishingly poor. Simply put, Swift never could accept a gift. While other men might find goodness manifested in a sunset sky or a starlit night, Swift seems never to have done so. Only when he could give something away did the world come fully alive for him. That is why Stella meant life itself to him; she depended on his life. The stars meant nothing at all.

Not to feel the stars shine is a deplorable condition, for it reflects a degree of pride that may in time separate its victim from his own life. Thus, it is just possible that, though he preached as a Christian for over three decades, Swift may have been too proud always fully to believe that God died for him. If this is true, however, it only means that, in order to be honest, Swift often had to preach pamphlets instead of sermons, and, in order to be "redeemed into life," he had to achieve a revivifying humility in some way other than an adamantine belief in Gospel.

On the evidence of the Stella poems, the way Swift found was charity. In charity to Stella, Swift did what he could not always do for himself; he brought a world to life through faith and hope. He not only exhibits the three theological virtues, but he also permits us to understand why charity is the greatest of those virtues. Offering his life to Stella, Swift found his life, and closing his last poem to her by asking her for charity—"Me, surely me, you ought to spare" (l. 83)—he gave and took the finest gift of all.

NOTES

1. See, for example, Sybil Le Brocquy's *Swift's Most Valuable Friend* (Dublin: Dolman Press, 1968), pp. 121–22, and also A. L. Rowse's *Jonathan Swift* (New York: Scribner's, 1975), pp. 198–99.

2. *The Correspondence of Jonathan Swift*, ed. Sir Harold Williams, 5 vols. (Oxford: Clarendon Press, 1965), 3: 236.

3. This statement may seem too bold, but I am thinking of my choices as eternal alternatives. See William James, *The Varieties of Religious Experience* (New York: Longmans, Green, 1916), pp. 140–44.

4. This view is too general to be attributed to any particular group of readers; for a recent and sensitive version see Robert W. Uphaus, "Swift's Stella Poems and Fidelity to Experience," *Eire-Ireland* 5 (1970): 40–52.

5. All quotations of Swift's poetry are from *The Poems of Jonathan Swift*, ed. Sir Harold Williams, 3 vols., 2d ed. (Oxford: Clarendon Press, 1958).

6. The material reviewed in the next two paragraphs is very common; see especially, however, Ludwig Edelstein, *The Meaning of Stoicism* (Cambridge, Mass.: Harvard University Press, 1966), pp. 90–98.

7

Notes on the Developing Motives and Structures of Swift's Poetry

RICHARD H. RODINO

College of the Holy Cross

Most of Swift's still widely read poems were written either in 1706–14 or in 1730–33. Preoccupation with the similarities between these two groups has produced the notion that Swift's verse is a homogeneous batch ("Swiftian"), thereby masking important differences and obscuring just how Swift developed as a poet.

The most significant differences are in the ways assertions are arranged and in the motives that may be inferred from these arrangements. Though modern criticism has pretty well established that eighteenth-century poetry was most notable for nonrational organization, Swift and Pope did not begin their careers thinking of this quality as a virtue in poetry.[1] To understand the motives of Swift's earliest poems, we need to recognize that Swift, as well as Pope, began writing poetry in the belief that certain verse structures had power to deal with the conflicting demands of idealism and honesty, without slighting either.[2] Swift found these structures in 1698, but he began looking for them in his very first poems.

In the early odes, idealism and honesty contend so strenuously that the poet's resources of accommodation boggled. Idealism (as hero worship) is progressively enervated by Swift's stubborn insistence that all the disjunctions between his heroes and the world they struggle to amend should be acknowledged. This process of enervation can be traced in the deteriorating relations between imagery and argument in the first three odes. In the "Ode to the King" (1690–91), Swift's imagery obscures disjunction in something like Dryden's early manner in *Astraea Redux*, in which images often appear in crammed succession. But in "Ode to the Athenian Society" (1692), Swift compares the strategies of "True Philosophy" to those of Proteus, "This Surly, *Slipp'ry God*"[3] (l. 197), and thereby exhibits through his imagery how even a presumably stable value may be controlled by the need to gratify the unvaluing mob. In his next ode, "To Sir William Temple" (1692), Swift attempts to confront the resistance of a nonheroic world to heroic virtue, power, and influence, but the crucial image of Temple's "garden," promising regeneration, is undercut by the fact that Swift himself (the manifest fruit of Temple's pastoral cultivation) finally ends his poem complaining about his own unfailing weediness.[4]

In "Ode to Sancroft" (1692), friction between image and statement degenerates by the close of the poem into an irresolvable clash of two voices: one asserting the immanence of divine, inscrutable wisdom; the other affirming the experience of practical, earthly frustrations. Equivocal imagery becomes contradictory argument. In "To Congreve" (1693) resolution of a sort is implicit in the angry satiric voice that constantly interrupts a voice merely stating the dilemma; the energy of the former at least hints of a breaking of the impasse. But in the last ode, "Occasioned by Sir William Temple's Late Illness and Recovery" (1693), Swift's muse consciously laments the reduction of poetic scale and subject in "To Congreve," and urges the young poet to revert to the themes and grand idealism of his first pindarics. The last lines of this final ode must have come hard for Swift. The madness and foolishness that he consistently opposed in earlier poems are identified in this one with his own, now disclaimed, idealism. The brilliant disintegrations of *A Tale of a Tub* naturally follow this unhappy conclusion to Swift's experiments in heroic verse.

But so does another, very different reaction: after a poetical silence of almost six years, Swift began writing verses structured according to accepted social and moral conventions. Each of these poems, written between 1698 and 1714, reflects one of two basic processes: balance and synthesis, or polarization and exclusion. These processes each suggest a different attitude toward a part of experience, but each does rely on shared rational standards that bind together the author of the poems and his readers, a bond important to see in the poems of this period if we are to understand what happens in Swift's later verse.[5]

Swift's first "sublunary" poem, "Verses wrote in a Lady's *Ivory Table-Book*" (1698) exhibits a process of balance and synthesis: effusive love lyrics and the silly obsessions of fashionable ladies are sandwiched between lines of hard-headed condemnation (ll. 1–6, 17–28). Swift nowhere describes a positive program of behavior, but, partly by its easy wittiness, the antithetical construction indicates an implicit ideal of moderation. The force of censure is qualified by the humor of the imagined scene; the harsh beginning and ending fortify the middle portion against its tendency to run to pure comedy. Overall, the effect is at once didactic and yet whimsical. The same sort of structure governs "To *Mrs.* Biddy Floyd" (1708), which alternates the large, ambiguous names of abstract virtues with the negative aspects such names contain and tend to conceal. The continuing act of discrimination moves toward an implicit synthesis, neatly and gracefully wrapped up in the last word: "Floyd."

These analyses themselves are commonplace, but I want to emphasize the tenor of mind these poems reveal: the commitment to normative values and orderly discriminations. These poems endorse analytical thought; the moral and even the social ethos can be made knowable by deliberate efforts to distinguish and to connect. Commitment to this sort of reasoning relies on a relatively unthreatened sense of moral value, even though the values themselves may be discoverable only through compromise.

Although most of Swift's poems about women from 1698 to 1714 are structured similarly, "Corinna" (1711) belongs to a second category of structures in which oppositions do not affirm a positive middle ground but rather devolve into genuine duality: virtuous love and ethical satire distort each other within Corinna's soul, creating an absurd and dangerous hybrid. Because defending purity is the principal motive of this kind of poetry, compromise is manifestly condemned; Corinna becomes that worst of women, "half Whore, half Wife" (l. 26). Often in poems of this kind Swift depends upon analogy, either for friendly instruction or merciless destruction. In the former case, he supplies his analogies without insisting on point-by-point correspondences, a procedure that allows him to defend complete and ideal values without falling into soul-searching complexities, as in the odes. "Atlas writt. 1712 to the Earl of Oxford" warns Harley about the dangers of not finding a worthy successor to his ministry; the imprecise language describing the political situation ("Premier Minister," "Weight of Kingdoms") refers back to the story of Atlas and Hercules without clouding the issues with the complications of actual events. "Verses *said to be written on the* Union" (1707) uses a series of analogies to illustrate the incongruity and danger of middle-ground concessions to the Presbyterian Scots. The very brevity of each successive analogy keeps the value of the union large and uninvestigated.[6] However, in attack there is often a progressive quality to Swift's analogies as the disparities between purity and compromise, or purity and distortion, are gradually revealed. The incongruity inherent in all metaphors—which subverted Swift's hero worship in his early odes—is now put to use thematically; one of the terms of comparison is made so incongruous, negates the other so thoroughly, that the connection must be totally rejected. Balance and compromise are present in these satires (e.g., "The Problem," "The Description of a Salamander") only to be subsequently excluded to establish a frame of reference so that unambiguous discriminations may be made.[7]

Both verse structures assume that the utility of art is connected to reasoned, analytical exercises of the mind, but the first kind is inclusive and conciliatory, while the second tends to work defensively, by exclusion and rejection. In both kinds of verse the speaker's tone is confident; he assumes no real difference in values between himself and his audience.

Particularly toward the end of his years in England, some of Swift's best-known poetry is governed by a third kind of structure. "A Description of the Morning" (1709) is serially arranged: a sequence of independent observations, controlled not by an intellectual or moral perspective, as in the case of the poems already discussed, but by spatial organization. The studied neglect of selection based on moral terms has interesting affinities to the elusive alternations of perspective in "Baucis and Philemon" (1706) and "A Description of a City Shower" (1710): also, these alternations neither point to clear norms nor give over wholeheartedly to parody. The potential of these largely additive, unjudging forms for self-inquiry is most evident in the remarkable poem Swift wrote just after his retirement from public affairs, "The Author Upon Himself" (1714). The tentative—sometimes playful, sometimes solemn, sometimes exaggeratedly horrified—constructions and reconstructions of attitudes in the poem emphasize the sheer difficulty of ascertaining ultimate causes and assigning genuine blame in the problematical world of political events.[8]

Many of these poems are products of a conspicuously sophisticated sensibility. Behind the cityscape of "A Description of the Morning," for instance, is an almost introspective fascination with the operation of the poet's own faculties of apprehension. Each couplet (endstopped, the metrical and grammatical units coinciding with a unit of observation) tends to detach itself from the others, and the alliteration holding each line together also helps to hold the individual lines apart as fragments. The poem, a series of details related essentially by the movement of an eye from inside the house to the streets of London, is not cumulative and progressive, but rather additive and successive. Its movement is linear, but causation is pretty much a mystery; details are added, but they do not add up to a coherent attitude. Similarly, the much-discussed "levels of meaning" in "City Shower" are not levels at all: they have a linear, not a superimposed, relationship.[9] By continuously varying his tone and angle of vision, Swift makes the process of judging the moral worth of what is described in this kind of poem a difficult and perhaps disconcerting one for his reader.

"Cadenus and Vanessa" (1713) is based on a similar motive. It imitates the first kind of structure discussed—a series of ironic reversals demonstrates that the false extremes of cold rationality and untempered passion are equally inadequate for the needs of complete human love. But here the "transcendent resolution" is deliberately made secret and private. The famous "cryptic passage" (ll. 818–27) reemphasizes that the problem cannot be solved by either reason or physical passion alone, but it does not suggest any way the two may be reconciled.[10]

Although Swift wrote half of all his poems during the years between 1714 and 1730, few of these are still read generally.

The poems to Stella are an exception, but by and large it is an undistinguished group, interesting and valuable mostly in what it tells about the important poems that preceded and followed it.

In writing about himself during this period, Swift makes (sometimes outrageous) claims for his own heroism, tests the waters of self-mockery, reasoned indignation, and thoughtful equanimity. If we summarize these turns, we find three major developments: Swift experimented both with modes of vindication and with modes of self-satire; his verse tends toward a balancing of perspectives and voices in the Horatian manner; and later poems become occasions to ponder the issue of "true Friendship," the theme of the most important poem he ever wrote.[11] These developments culminate in the poem Swift finished early in 1731, "The Life and Genuine Character of Doctor *Swift*," in which two speakers alternate defense and praise of Swift with criticism and attack. Perhaps most important, both speakers are deliberately named as "friends," and the "proem" is all about the differences between true and specious friendship.

Since "The Life and Genuine Character" really is a *terminus ad quem* of the direction Swift's poems about himself were taking by 1730–31, it is highly significant that he so vehemently repudiated the poem.[12] For just about this time Swift's motives were changing in all his poetry, and the rather effective Horatian apologia was no longer satisfying. Why did Swift so completely prefer "Verses on the Death of Dr. *Swift*"? Arthur H. Scouten and Robert D. Hume settled a long critical debate over the structure of the poem by demonstrating that the eulogy is "neither pure apologia nor pure irony."[13] However, the question of motive remains. In the structure of the poem, the eulogy is that part which demonstrates the truth of what Swift argued in the first part. And it does this in an unusually cunning and ruthless way. At the beginning of the poem, Swift tells us that equals, hero-worshipers, and poets are driven to envy by the successes of others. The eulogy deliberately flaunts the successes, piety, and greatness of Swift's life before his "Equals"; it flaunts his heroism before those in Ireland who are obligated to him; and it flaunts the noble motives and universal popularity of his writings before "Brethren Poets." The eulogy traps the reader into feeling the resentful envy predicted by the first part of the poem, thereby proving as true what had seemed at first to be an outrageous attack on human nature.

Another example of how Swift's motives changed in the early 1730s is the way he used animal imagery and fables. Between "Baucis and Philemon" (1706) and "The Beasts Confession to the Priest" (1732), these images are used to suggest that animal behavior consistently defines human vice and folly (except for the traditional superior loyalty of the Dog in "The Dog and the Thief"). In his fables Swift accepted the basic assumptions of the "orthodox" English fable, articulated by John Dennis: limited and unequivocal application; precedence of moral over story.[14]

Early in his career, and again after 1730, Swift perceived the dangers of fables in terms precisely opposite to those which underlie his poems of 1714–30. Nothing is more comforting than thinking that vice is simply a deviation from the natural virtuousness of man—a presumption reinforced by dualistic fable structures and by the use of animals as images of human feelings. By 1730 there are signs that Swift revived his contempt for the direct applications of animal fables. His reply to Delany's tale of "The Pheasant and the Lark &c." begins by deriding the very idea of applying a reductive fable to the complexities of a modern situation. It is a fact that by 1730 Swift himself had abandoned sincere fables forever; he found a more excruciating satiric power in turning the premise of fables upside down in "On Poetry: A *Rapsody*" and in the conclusion to "The Beasts Confession to the Priest," asserting that the natural virtue and harmony of animals is everything that man is not.[15] "The Beasts Confession" especially is motivated by a desire to "vex" the reader rather than to teach or to delight him. The two parts of the poem (ll. 1–196, 197–220), taken separately, amount to two conventional satires. The long fable (ll. 1–196) denounces abuses of reason (when man lowers himself to the level of beasts), in the manner of Boileau or even the much-despised L'Estrange.[16] The second part (ll. 197-220) is a vituperative declaration that man is not possessed of reason at all, in the manner of Rochester, or Robert Gould, or William Wycherley. But the structure of the poem as a whole goes beyond either kind of satire by the suddenness with which it juxtaposes the two contradictory satiric assumptions, the unconcern with which the second part announces that the premises of the first part are false and delusory. Swift spends almost two hundred lines writing exactly the sort of animal fable that the remainder of the poem denounces.

The most unexpected thing about "The Beasts Confession" is that the voice urging us to "Apply the Tale" (l. 73) is every bit as straightforward and sincere as the voice that repudiates the application. Swift is altogether nonchalant about his rather staggering duplicity, not even wickedly pleased with himself for deceiving us. He seems unconcerned that he has broken an elemental rule of fable-telling: not only is the tale fraudulent, but the readers are not let in on the joke. The structure of conventional fables, along with the standard premise that beasts exemplify human sins, represents a normative position, a way of understanding the world in moral terms. Swift spends one hundred ninety-six lines convincing us to affirm this position and then sweeps it out from under us. His offhanded admission of inveracity seems calculated to estrange and dislocate rather than to enlighten. Swift does not try to *explain* how literary conventions tend dangerously to promote self-satisfaction; he exploits them primarily to *annoy* his readers.

Swift's poems about women show a parallel development, again climaxing in a radical change of strategy during the early 1730s. Between the "private" resolution of "Cadenus and Vanessa" and the vexatious scatological poems of 1730–32, Swift wrote a short series of "moral tales" about women and marriage. The typical manner of these poems, including "Phillis, Or, the Progress of Love" (1719) and "The Progress of Marriage" (1722), is to make early and complete distinctions, with unambiguous invitations to the reader to share Swift's comic and wholesome overview.[17] The exception is "The Progress of Beauty" (1719), which prefigures the concentration of "vexatious" poems in the early 1730s. The last ten stanzas of "The Progress of Beauty" parody Swift's earlier structure of balance and reconciliation, pretending to work through a problem of specious extremes only to end up making the middle ground just as unappetizing. The unexpected solution to this tragic predicament is the speaker's detached and chilling indifference: inhuman and stingingly irrelevant.

"The Lady's Dressing Room" (1730) is equally vexing. In the closing lines the plausible and ingratiating speaker startles us with his sudden relish for "stinking Ooze," a "pocky Quean," "gaudy Tulips rais'd from Dung" (ll. 132, 134, 144); the only requirement for enjoying these things is that one hold one's nose. The speaker's scorn of Strephon's fastidiousness conceals his own repellent grossness. Just as in "The Beasts Confession," we are lured into complacency in order to be made thoroughly uncomfortable about the opinions we have easily assumed.

In different ways, "A Beautiful Young Nymph Going to Bed" (1731) and "Strephon and Chloe" (1731) are also structured to deny us firm footing among the dilemmas they describe. As in Gulliver's last voyage or "A Digression Concerning Madness," we are deluded into making impossible, but seemingly urgent, choices among fraudulent alternatives. In the "vexatious" poems all the alternatives seem repulsive, and we are meant to feel just this sort of dislocation. "The Day of Judgement" (1731?) strips away the comforting props of religious formulae from everyone through Jove's biting indifference to what human beings expect in the way of orderly reward and punishment. After the pounding condemnation of the first fourteen lines of "The Place of the Damn'd" (1731), the reader is only too glad to arrive at what seems to be a safe retreat into the moralizing of lines 15-18. But he is actually led into a snare of self-righteous complacency ("*HELL* to be sure is at *Paris* or *Rome*"). The abrupt shift from a cynical *j'accuse* to a deliberately obtuse voice, pretending to represent the reader's point of view, promises relief, then snatches it away.[18]

The motives of "The Legion Club" (1736), Swift's last significant work, are more complex than would at first appear. In a sense it is at once more engaged and more hopeless than the "vexatious" poems, a gesture of compulsive concern, without hope of reforming, or redeeming, or finally even of fending off its enemies. The hopelessness is even more frightening than the mocking, but controlled, traps of the earlier poems. Swift had been worrying about the problem of literary action in the face of irredeemable corruption between 1733 and 1736, as in his letter of April 1733 about wit in satire: "it will onely serve to vex Rogues, though it will not amend them."[19] The need to hurt, in the absence of a more helpful motive, is documented in "The Legion Club" in Swift's advice to the Keeper: "Lash them daily, lash them duly,/Though 'tis hopeless to reclaim them" (ll. 156-57).

But these lines represent only one stage in a poem devoted to exploring the possibilities of literary action; in particular, the poem is a recapitulation of Swift's own poetic career. It begins with a sense of normative values and moral dualism: the activity of strolling the city and the reassuring presence of the College ("Sense and Knowledge," l. 4) are both posed against the absurd but dangerous House of Commons. The "prudent Architect" (l. 5) seems to cooperate, satirically placing the demonic pile "against" (l. 6) the Church. The world outside the "Legion Club" seems at first to be allied against the idiocy within, and the speaker's voice is sane in its denunciation. But he pushes too far into invective (by ll. 63-74 his "expedient" becomes merely a catalogue of insults), which becomes self-defeating, and he must be pulled back by his Muse, who argues for scorn rather than anger, contempt rather than violence. The Muse's guided tour through hellish Parliament momentarily calms what was nearly a lunatic frenzy, and the speaker begins again in a new key, hatred buried for a moment in amazement at the perverse wonderland that imagination can sometimes make out of the despicable.

When finally abandoned by the Muse, the speaker carries on as best he can, his concern for his ideals breaking through his manufactured hard shell of uncaring. Surrounded by overwhelming inhumanity, unable entirely to control his sadness, he reminds himself of the reward in "laughing with a few friends [such as Hogarth] in a corner," but even this sort of escape is now a fleeting comfort for the mature poet. The poem ends with a full retreat into "silence," after a curiously half-hearted curse, as if there were no point even to that.[20]

"The Legion Club" is a fitting rehearsal of Swift's lifelong unwillingness to glamorize literary resolutions and the deception they breed. In the irredeemable world of "The Legion Club," not much is left finally but the memory of the striving integrity of a single voice, now rather pathetic. This bitter and depressing end to Swift's career is a hard fact to swallow for those who like to think of Swift as a Christian poet or even a moralist. But the later years of his career are full of extreme measures in the name of honesty, and "The Legion Club" reminds us at the most disconcerting level that the "victories" of satire are painfully unlike material reform. At the end of his career, Swift had no convenient myth of order or of transcendent "self" to interpose between himself and the world recorded by his senses and his imagination.

NOTES

1. See, for example, D. J. Greene, " 'Logical Structure' in Eighteenth-Century Poetry," *Philological Quarterly* 31 (1952): 315-36; Ralph Cohen, "The Augustan Mode in English Poetry," *Studies in the Eighteenth Century*, ed. R. F. Brissenden (Toronto: University of Toronto Press, 1968), pp. 171-92; Peter Thorpe, "The Nonstructure of Augustan Verse," *Papers on Language and Literature* 5 (1969): 235-51; Morris Golden, *The Self Observed: Swift, Johnson, Wordsworth* (Baltimore, Md.: Johns Hopkins Press, 1972); C. J. Rawson, "Order and Misrule: Eighteenth-Century Literature in the 1970's," *English Literary History* 42 (1975): 471-505; A. B. England, "World Without Order: Some Thoughts on the Poetry of Swift," *Essays in Criticism* 16 (1966): 32-43.

2. With respect to Pope see Thomas R. Edwards, Jr., *This Dark Estate: A Reading of Pope*, Perspectives in Criticism, no. 11 (Berkeley: University of California Press, 1963).

3. All quotations of Swift's poetry are from *The Poems of Jonathan Swift*, ed. Sir Harold Williams, 3 vols., 2d ed. (Oxford: Clarendon Press, 1958).

4. See Kathryn Montgomery Harris, " 'Occasions so Few': Satire as a Strategy of Praise in Swift's Early Odes," *Modern Language Quarterly* 31 (1970): 28.

5. These two categories resemble Ronald Paulson's "Whig" and "Tory." See *The Fictions of Satire* (Baltimore, Md.: Johns Hopkins Press, 1967), especially pp. 210-22.

6. C. J. Rawson discusses the importance of brevity in Swift's satire in "Order and Cruelty: Swift, Pope and Johnson," *Gulliver and the Gentle Reader: Studies in Swift and Our Time* (London: Routledge and Kegan Paul, 1973), p. 34.

7. A. B. England discusses a few poems of this kind in "The Subversion of Logic in Some Poems by Swift," *Studies in English Literature* 15 (1975): 409-18, with somewhat different conclusions, though we disagree less than his title might suggest.

8. Thomas R. Edwards, Jr., discusses similar strategies in *An Essay on Man* in "Visible Poetry: Pope and Modern Criticism," *Harvard English Studies*, ed. Reuben A. Brower (Cambridge, Mass.: Harvard University Press, 1971), 2: 299-321.

9. See F. W. Bateson, "A Description of the Morning," *English Poetry: A Critical Introduction* (London: Longmans, Green and Co., 1950), p. 176; Cohen, "The Augustan Mode," pp. 174-75.

10. See Richard Hodge Rodino, "The Private Sense of *Cadenus and Vanessa*," *Concerning Poetry* 11, no. 2 (Fall 1978): 41-47.

11. The poems I have in mind include, in the first case, "Horace, *Lib. 2, Sat.* 6" (1714), "Traulus, the First Part" (1730), "On the Irish-Club" (1730), "A Dialogue Between an Eminent Lawyer and Dr. *Swift*" (1730), and "A Panegyrick on the Dean

in the Person of a Lady in the *North*" (1730); in the second case, "A Dialogue," "A Panegyrick," and the two parts of "Traulus"; in the third the series of poems Swift wrote revolving around Delany's suit to Lord Carteret, particularly "A Libel on Doctor Delany and a Certain Great Lord." This last poem seems especially logical and orderly in structure, but it is not so straightforward as it seems. The heady praise in the portrait of Pope (ll. 71-88) is a sort of prototype of the eulogy on Swift himself in his verses on his own death. Other poems about "true Friendship" in 1730 are "The Dean's Reasons" and "A Panegyrick on the Dean in the Person of a Lady in the *North*."

12. *The Correspondence of Jonathan Swift*, ed. Sir Harold Williams, 5 vols. (Oxford: Clarendon Press, 1965), 4: 149, 151, 161. Hereafter cited as *Corr.*

13. "Pope and Swift: Text and Interpretation of Swift's Verses on His Death," *Philological Quarterly* 52 (1973): 205-31; disagreements about the poem and possible approaches to interpretation are analyzed by David M. Vieth, "The Mystery of Personal Identity: Swift's Verses on His Own Death," *The Author in His Work: Essays on a Problem in Criticism*, ed. Louis L. Martz and Aubrey Williams (New Haven, Conn.: Yale University Press, 1978), pp. 245-62.

14. See, for example, *The Critical Works of John Dennis*, ed. Edward Niles Hooker (Baltimore, Md.: Johns Hopkins Press, 1943), 1: 56-57; 2: 110, 138.

15. In 1732, when Gay was writing the sequel to his own *Fables*, he suspected that Swift did not approve. Swift wrote back to smooth Gay's ruffled feathers, but at the same time he made his own disavowal explicit: "I remember, I acted as you seem to hint, I found a moral first, & studied for a Fable, but cou'd do nothing that pleased me, & so left off that scheme forever," *Corr.*, 4: 38-39.

16. L'Estrange, *Fables, of Aesop and other Eminent Mythologists: with Morals and Reflexions* (London: R. Sage, 1694); *Fables and Storyes Moralized. Being a Second Part of the Fables of Aesop and Other Eminent Mythologists, &c.* (London: R. Sage, 1699).

17. See my much longer discussion of these poems in "Blasphemy or Blessing? Swift's 'Scatological' Poems," *Papers on Language and Literature* 14 (1978): 152-70.

18. See Maurice Johnson, *The Sin of Wit: Jonathan Swift as a Poet* (Syracuse, N.Y.: Syracuse University Press, 1950), p. 79.

19. *Corr.*, 4: 138.

20. By "silence" I mean something like the act George Steiner describes: "It is better for the poet to mutilate his own tongue than to dignify the inhuman either with his gift or his uncaring." *Language and Silence: Essays on Language, Literature, and the Inhuman* (New York: Atheneum, 1967), p. 54.

8

Fictive Self-Portraiture in Swift's Poetry

LOUISE K. BARNETT

Rutgers University

When an author names a character after himself, he introduces a biographical dimension into his work; the critic must come to terms with it or ignore an overt and essential aspect of the literary text. In his discussion of Pope's epistles Maynard Mack provides an approach to the problem of biography with his suggestion that a first-person speaker identified with the author can be a rhetorical strategy, necessary to establish a "satirical ethos."[1] If the satirist does not appear to be a particular kind of person, exhibiting—as Pope claims for himself—the strong antipathy of good to bad, his satire will lack credibility. Useful as this model is for many satiric speakers, it cannot be applied to the major part of Swift's poetry of fictive self-portraiture. From the earliest ventures on, Swift's depiction of self lacks the dichotomized presentation of good opposing bad that is essential to the satiric speaker. The self is both exalted and ridiculed within a full spectrum of character possibilities that includes the satirist-hero at one extreme and the unscrupulous opportunist at the other. In Swift's poetry self tends to be its own end rather than a strategy for presenting something else.

From first to last, Swift's poetry exemplifies what Maurice Johnson has called "the biographical presence."[2] Even in his first poems, officially committed to the praise of others, self often displaces the putative subject. In the chronological development of Swift's poetry, poems that are primarily concerned with a fictive Swift assume increasing prominence, as if with growing maturity and skill the poet felt less hesitant to admit that he was his own best subject and more engrossed with the possibilities he discovered in fictive self-portraiture.

Swift's treatment of self in his earliest poetry shows a struggle to find his own poetic voice within the constraints of the pindaric ode. His ambivalent feelings, split not only between poetry and a worldly career but between more elevated genres and satire, are expressed in the form of a quarrel with his muse. Although the odes are intended to be panegyrics, they are chiefly memorable as the record of Swift's developing self-discovery. By the final ode Swift can renounce the subterfuge of the muse because he has clarified his attitude toward poetry and is now willing to assert his preference for fictive self-portraiture and satire.

The next stage is to treat different versions of self in separate poems, some of which use the same occasion to construct dissimilar portraits, as if Swift is trying out different interpretations of the same data. "My Lady's Lamentation and Complaint against the Dean" criticizes the same behavior extolled in "A Panegyrick on the Dean"; "The Author upon Himself" portrays a politically influential Swift, an interpretation that is then challenged by "Horace, *Lib.* 2 *Sat.* 6."[3]

Swift's poetry of fictive self-portraiture culminates in "The Life and Genuine Character of Dr. Swift" and "Verses on the Death of Dr. Swift" with the presentation in each of conflicting portraits within the same poem. These are Swift's most ambitious ventures and greatest achievements in fictive self-portraiture—attempts to construct a fictive self for posterity by reworking the diverse materials that constitute public opinion.

Although Swift is a poet who responds to occasions furnished by the world, from national issues like the Wood's Patent controversy to events of personal significance like Stella's birthday, underneath the specific impetus is an ongoing desire to create self-portraits in poetry. When Swift is not writing about Swift third person or speaking as Swift first person, he is devising other ways of making himself the subject, most commonly by inventing some other character—often a fictive version of a real person—whose theme is Swift. Thus, a "Lady in the North" (Lady Acheson) writes "A Panegyrick on the Dean," while Lewis and Harley, political figures and friends of Swift, describe and discuss him in "Part of the Seventh Epistle of the First Book of Horace Imitated." Reporting other people's opinions of himself, rather than allowing *them* to speak, is another of the poet's favorite techniques for introducing the subject of self. "The Author upon Himself," whose title suggests that it will be Swift on Swift, is actually a report of the judgments of others about him. Purportedly external comment, often made by unidentifiable speakers, runs the gamut from extravagant praise through neutral statement to scorn and condemnation. The credentials, if any, of these disembodied voices—and hence the reliability of their pronouncements—are difficult to determine.

These multiple self-portraits are partial views that add up to a total, multifaceted view of Swift's relations with women, disciples, servants, ministers, friends, enemies, public opinion, and posterity. When Swift constructs idealistic portraits, even such astute and friendly readers as Pope have been made uncomfortable; when instead he becomes a figure of fun in his poetry there is less puzzlement, for we conventionally approve the man who can laugh at himself.[4] Truly ignoble portraits also exist, one drawn so convincingly that it was anonymously published by an unfriendly printer as an authentic libel.[5] Behind the profusion of perspectives on self in Swift's poetry lies a modern sense of the mosaic of human personality, motivation, and perception—an awareness of and interest in the complexity of the self. Swift's poetry of fictive self-portraiture focuses upon the closest and yet the most intractable of materials—the poet's own experience and psyche, the most available and compelling example of that problematical entity, human nature.

Since role tends to determine the kind of portrait or portraits Swift constructs, a useful approach to this body of poetry is to group poems according to the role the character of Swift plays. Most of the Market Hill poems, for example, originate in Swift's violations of the role of guest, comically juxtaposed to his hostess's imprisonment within the conventions of hospitality. In the poems written for Stella's birthday, Swift plays ironically contrasting roles: vulnerably human but also artistically powerful, he is both the man who depends upon Stella's friendship and care and the poet who preserves her merit in art. Rather than such private versions of self, other poems present Swift as writer, politician, churchman—in other words, as a public man. These poems work with the disparate views that make up the reputation of a well-known figure and are consequently more complex than the poems of the private self.

Whatever their distance from the reality of Swift's life, his fictive selves assume the guise and authority of biography. The identity of author and character in "The Author upon Himself" and "Horace, *Lib*. 2. *Sat*. 6." and the common biographical basis—that the man described is known to be a real person who did associate with Harley and Bolingbroke—give the poems a certain degree of credibility.

But where they diverge in their treatment of Swift's political role (real power versus sham), art, not biography, must provide the resolution.

The abiding concern of Swift's poetry of fictive self-portraiture is not to lead back to biography through the expression of a "real self," but to refract and thus meditate upon the world's perceptions and misperceptions of this self. As Swift wrote to Bolingbroke and Pope: "[I wanted to] be used like a Lord by those who have an opinion of my parts; *whether right or wrong, it is no great matter*"[6] (emphasis added). Views of the self are almost always filtered through other imagined consciousnesses because Swift is not writing confessions but constructing portraits that are always to some degree public and external. The two self-portraits offered by "The Author upon Himself" and "Horace, *Lib. 2. Sat. 6.*" resonate against the historical public figure of Swift to form a triptych—multiple interpretations that exemplify the difficulty of measuring the kind of unofficial, behind-the-scenes position Swift held. Such different perspectives on the same events illustrate the variety and fallibility of opinion; further, they suggest that there may be no definitive judgment possible. What the pairing of the poems insists upon is an issue of evaluation: the same set of facts, the general public knowledge of Swift's political career, can yield radically different interpretations.

Swift's use of multiple self-portraits in his poetry is similar to the procedure he recommended for pursuing political truth: "Whoever has so little to do as to desire some Knowledge in Secrets of State, must compare what he hears from severall great men, or from one great man at severall Times, which is equally different."[7] The conflicting views of Swift suggest a number of possibilities—a split between a distorted public image, the product of irresponsible gossip, and the truth; between an unattainable ideal and a flawed reality; between the polarized images created by interested parties, friends and enemies, or by different vantage points, cynical outsider and sympathetic insider. Labeling all portraits "Swift" is a compelling dramatic device to provoke these reflections.

However data may be classified biographically—and its range includes fact, half-truth, untruth, conjecture, and fantasy, in the poetry it must be regarded as fictive statement, part of a created context rather than history. Swift's most characteristic use of biographical materials is neither a straightforward presentation of truth nor a mechanical reversal of fictive to true. It is subtle, ambiguous, ultimately impossible to categorize precisely because no one formula of relationship is sustained for long.

Portraits of the public man in Swift's poetry are usually posited upon the kind of general knowledge of Swift that an average contemporary reader might be expected to have. When Swift's subject is a more private version of self than this well-known figure, the poetry contains enough conventional clues to guide the reader. Even such personal portraits of Swift as the Market Hill poems construct are accessible without their implicit biographical *donnée*, the close friendship of the Achesons and the Dean. When Lady Acheson extols Swift's preaching in "A Panegyrick on the Dean," Swift's note informs the reader that he "preached but once while he was there." In the same poem the praise of Swift for serving as butler would be correctly read as humorous deprecation even without Swift's note that "he sometimes used to direct the Butler."[8]

The poems undoubtedly contain private biographical jokes designed for limited audiences, but when these are discovered they invariably enhance rather than alter the poetic statement. Knowing that Swift could be cantankerous transforms an inert detail in "Verses on the Death of Dr. Swift"—"was chearful to his dying Day"—into a joke, but by this point in the poem (l. 477) the reader should already suspect that the dubious locale where the eulogy is delivered and the extravagant absolute claims made for Swift signalize irony.[9]

Perhaps most significant of Swift's reasons for writing his poetry of fictive self-portraiture is the desire to leave a record of himself to combat what he described in the "Ode to the Athenian Society" as "Careless and Ignorant Posterity" (l. 163). In some part Swift may have wanted to "turn private crisis into public example,"[10] as Geoffrey Hill suggests, but in the main his self-absorption seems more personal, more a question of mastering private crisis by establishing his own version of it. By controlling in art what he knew could not be controlled in reality, Swift could exorcise those threats to the self that he found so fearful, those judgments—whether malicious, uninformed, or merely imagined—which gave him less than his due. Swift's poetry of fictive self-portraiture is a response to what Robert C. Elliott calls the satirist's "primordial demand"[11] for overcoming, through ordering and controlling within the verbal universe of his art, those fears and confusions inspired by the self's troubling encounters not only with the world but with its own spirit as well.

Swift's autobiographical prose fragment, "Family of Swift," his correspondence, and Irvin Ehrenpreis's admirable biography, *Swift: the Man, his Works, and the Age,* document Swift's unhappiness at his ultimate failure to establish himself in the world. This controlling vision of his life has its counterpart in the major body of Swift's poems of fictive self-portraiture, poems that exhibit what I call strategies of self-defense directed against threats to the self. The intention of these poems is to defend the self from a multitude of real or imagined threats that can be exorcized by being confronted and mastered within an aesthetic construct. Typically, the self is shown under attack by a powerful opponent, either public opinion or an individual with social or political superiority to Swift. The characteristic structure of such a poem is a dialectical clash between opposing versions of Swift, in which techniques of indirection work against both positive and negative portraits. Overt ridicule and condemnation of Swift may be countered by indirectly expressed admiration or by the subtle discrediting of an anti-Swift speaker, while praise of Swift may be undercut by irony or called into question by flagrant hyperbole. But invariably the movement of the poetic structure is toward the revelation of Swift as a sympathetic figure.

In the Market Hill poems, for example, the esteemed friend and welcome guest that Swift historically was is transmuted into a fictive opposite. A hostile speaker, often Lady Acheson, reacts to Swift's behavior with indignation and mockery but is always exposed as unreliable. The caricatures of ill-behaved guest and mean-spirited hostess are broad comic types, but the issues of perception and judgment that the poems raise are serious: is the reported behavior of Swift unmannerly and officious or helpful and considerate? As is so often the case, Swift's use of biographical material in these fictive versions of self diminishes its factuality and stresses the importance of the evaluative process rather than the data. That Swift enjoyed taking on projects around the estate and instructing Lady Acheson are facts that, depending on point of view, may be interpreted as gestures of friendly interest or presumptuous usurpations. The negative constructions placed upon Swift's actions by Lady Acheson are all possibilities that could be actualized within the real Swift-Acheson friendship or within any friendship through a failure of communication or a difference of opinion. Fictive Swift embodies those aggravating and embarrassing characteristics that the poet may perceive as exaggerations of his real tendencies or unfriendly misconstructions of his behavior by others. By naming these deficiencies himself, turning them into jokes within his own poetry, he demonstrates power over them and exorcizes their threat. Moreover, it is only on the surface that Swift is mocked. Those who see him critically are themselves discredited, for while the poems show that Swift has tried to help the inhabitants of Market Hill in numerous ways, they have resisted his good intentions and relished thoughts of his humiliation. The revelation of Swift as morally superior to his antagonists completes the strategy of self-defense.

All of the poetry of fictive self-portraiture reveals a vulnerability to forces that the poet cannot control in the world outside his poem—time, death, and above all, slander. The fictive Swifts call to mind the world of flux and misfortune that Swift the man has no choice but to live in. This world both occasions and intrudes into the poetic universe; terrifying possibilities are conjured up and then overcome through the resources of the poet's art.[12] In the short poem "Drapier's Hill," for example, listing the various tokens of his greatest public triumph is both a loving commemoration and a fearful encounter, for Swift imagines the worst, the total obliteration of all these gratifying memorials:

> That when a Nation long enslav'd,
> Forgets by whom it once was sav'd,
> When none the DRAPIER's Praise shall sing;
> His Signs aloft no longer swing;
> His Medals and his Prints forgotten,
> And all his Handkerchiefs are rotten;
> His famous LETTERS made waste Paper.
> (ll. 11-17)

Anticipating the evils of time and malice, Swift prepares to counter them in advance by making his property a monument, which is then preserved in poetry:

> This Hill may keep the Name of Drapier:
> In Spight of Envy flourish still,
> And Drapier's vye with Cooper's Hill.
>
> (ll. 18-20)

Reputation may be attacked or forgotten, but the poet exorcizes these threats to the self by preserving his cherished victory in land and in poetry.

Swift's greatest work of fictive self-portraiture, "Verses on the Death of Dr. Swift," makes essentially the same statement. Like other men, Swift is shown to be prey to time, death, the distortions of malicious tongues, and his own weaknesses. Nevertheless, in Swift's view he is less vulnerable when he can exorcise those destructive phenomena, including his own egotism, by creating a poetic world to order and contain them. Like Yeats in "Sailing to Byantium," Swift escapes from the present not only through the process of making poetry, but through identifying the self with the artifact it has created. Yeats wishes to become the perfect aesthetic object, the golden bird. Swift cannot relinquish the self so completely, although he, too, wants to encompass past, present, and future by becoming the monument he has himself constructed for posterity—the poetic memorial to self.

NOTES

1. "The Muse of Satire," *The Yale Review* 41 (1951): 88.

2. "Swift's Poetry Reconsidered," *English Writers of the Eighteenth Century,* ed. John H. Middendorf (New York: Columbia University Press, 1971), p. 248.

3. All references to and citations of Swift's poetry are taken from *The Poems of Jonathan Swift,* ed. Sir Harold Williams, 3 vols., 2d ed. (Oxford: Clarendon Press, 1958).

4. The criticism of "Verses on the Death of Dr. Swift" is an excellent illustration of this difference in attitude. While little attention has been paid to the first two-thirds of the poem, where Swift is a ridiculed or ignored figure, from Pope on commentators have focused on the "eulogy" as the key to the poem's interpretation and the source of critical problems.

5. As Swift wrote to Lord Bathurst, Oct. 1730: "For, having some months ago much & often offended the ruling party, and often worryed by Libellers I am at the pains of writing one in their style & manner, & sent it by an unknown hand to a Whig printer who very faithfully published it." *The Correspondence of Jonathan Swift*, ed. Sir Harold Williams, 5 vols. (Oxford: Clarendon Press, 1953), 3: 410; see also 3: 418. Hereafter cited as *Corr.*

Following Sir Harold Williams's attribution, scholars—including myself—assumed that the poem referred to was "A Panegyric on the Reverend Dean *Swift*" (1730). At the 1977 Modern Language Association special session on Swift's poetry, Aubrey L. Williams pointed out that nowhere else in his writings does Swift treat himself as harshly as the "Panegyric" does. Primarily on the basis of internal evidence, Williams made a convincing case against Swift's authorship of the poem and suggested that the "Panegyric" was more likely to be the work of James Arbuckle. In light of this new doubt cast upon the poem, I have eliminated the several references to the "Panegyric" that the original version of my essay (given as a paper in the 1977 MLA special session) contained.

6. *Corr.*, 3: 330–31.

7. *Corr.*, 1: 185.

8. Faulkner's notes from the original publication of the poem in the 1735 *Miscellanies* are reproduced by Williams, *Poems*, 3: 888, n. 61 and 889, n. 88.

9. Peter J. Schakel, "The Politics of Opposition in 'Verses on the Death of Dr. Swift,' " *Modern Language Quarterly* 35 (1974): 247, offers evidence that the Rose Tavern was a disreputable political meeting place in Swift's time.

10. "Jonathan Swift: The Poetry of 'Reaction,' " *The World of Jonathan Swift: Essays for the Tercentenary*, ed. Brian Vickers (Cambridge, Mass.: Harvard University Press, 1968), p. 196.

11. See *The Power of Satire: Magic, Ritual, Art* (Princeton, N.J.: Princeton University Press, 1969), p. 58.

12. Not all of the poems of fictive self-portraiture succeed in mastering the opponent. "Cadenus and Vanessa," "Holyhead," and "*Stella's* Birth-Day *March* 13. 1726–7" are notable failures to overcome diverse threats to the self.

9

Autobiography in Swift's Verses on His Death

JAMES WOOLLEY

Lafayette College

From the time criticism of "Verses on the Death of Dr. Swift" began—with William King in 1739—its most significant effort has been to show that there is a discrepancy between what Swift said and what he meant, or should have meant, or should have said. Of the inventories and explanations of these discrepancies, probably those appearing under the rubric of irony have had the greatest appeal; and related explanations, discussing the eulogist's character, the poet's delight in various self-presentations, or his activity as a maker of myths or hoaxes, have recently assumed importance. But these essays have often labeled passages as inaccurate or ironic without inquiring closely enough into what an accurate or straightforward statement from Swift on the same subject would have been. This critical tradition has thus not been very useful to those who wish to pursue the biographical interest of "Verses on the Death."

We may surmise that the poem's rhetorical lapses, surveyed by Irvin Ehrenpreis, result from a conflict between the writer and his invented character, the eulogist.[1] On the one hand, there is a character who praises Swift—a character decorously distanced from him and free to exaggerate and generalize. On the other hand, there is Swift: unwilling to confine himself behind that mask, he emerges with sentiments that apparently embody his personal point of view, and with factual details that embarrass the generalizing tendency of the eulogy. When Swift seems to speak *in propria persona* he is often unconvincing, to say no worse. Yet we thereby get a revealing view of him, which is, after all, what the poem has encouraged us to want. We want to know what sense of himself permitted Swift to satirize others, and our curiosity is the more intense because we know it is risky for a satirist to permit too close a view of himself: he is, like his victims, only mortal.

Swift's willingness to disregard his rhetoric and to sacrifice the appearance of decorum that a more coherently maintained fictional character might have offered attests the importance he attached, at some level of his consciousness, to saying something about himself, and it encourages the reader to scrutinize the *closeness* of what Swift says to what he probably believed about himself. Commentators on the poem have often stressed Swift's inaccuracies as an objective historian. But for the critic interested in the quality of Swift's subjectivity, it is profitable to leave the question of accuracy very largely aside, and to compare statements in the poem with other statements—mainly in his letters—which presumably respond straightforwardly to contexts like those the poem refers to.[2]

In theory this comparison poses no obstacle to an ironic reading of the eulogy: some critics may prefer to stress differences between what Swift says and what he means, while I prefer to stress similarities. Practically speaking, however, this reading would oppose or at any rate markedly limit certain specific ironic interpretations that have been offered. It is not my purpose to deny that any behavior can be regarded as a front, or to argue that in the eulogy we have *the* real Jonathan Swift. But when a person talks about his past, he will often simplify and intensify his story by making generalizations absolute. If we look with sympathy behind the reduction, hyperbole, and clarification natural to character-writing and eulogy, we get a view of Swift that he himself took seriously—that is, one that he used repeatedly and straightforwardly elsewhere in describing some of the most important circumstances of his life.

The account of Swift as courtier and patron provides one specific instance of such self-characterization. The eulogy says that "the Dean, if we believe Report,/Was never ill receiv'd at Court" (ll. 307-8). While this claim has been doubted, we find Swift making it elsewhere. He writes to Archbishop King in 1711, "I am as well received and known at Court, as perhaps any man ever was of my Level; I have formerly been the like." And to Francis Grant he remarks in 1733, "I am out of favour at Court, where I was well received, during two summers, six or seven years ago."[3] Swift's recognition at court is a testimony of his merit (he cannot shake the notion that the Crown is the fount of honor, or ought to be). But when he finds himself out of favor, it is due to Caroline and Lady Suffolk's treachery and ingratitude, or so he is willing to believe. There is no necessary contradiction here.

As for what motivated Swift's courtly behavior, the eulogist in his hyperbolic way tells us that "Power was never in his Thought;/And, Wealth he valu'd not a Groat" (ll. 357-58). These lines occur in a passage arguing that Swift was careful not to form alliances of dependency that could jeopardize his principles. While he can resent not having achieved greater recognition in the world, he prides himself, he tells us through the eulogist, upon not having sacrificed his principles or his friends to gain wealth or power (ll. 355-64). Moreover, the passage is substantiated in Swift's preface to *The History of the Four Last Years of the Queen*: "I was so far from having any obligations to the crown, that, on the contrary, her Majesty issued a proclamation, offering 300 l. to any person who would discover the author of a certain short treatise, which the Queen well knew to have been written by me. I never received one shilling from the minister, or any other present, except that of a few books; nor did I want their assistance to support me. . . . I absolutely refused to be chaplain to the Lord Treasurer; because I thought it would ill become me to be in a state of dependence."[4]

It is likely that Swift exercised great self-discipline to over-come strong temptations: certainly the desirability of wealth and power entered his thought; certainly, too, he knew his disinclination to remain "chearful to his dying Day" (l. 477); and to the extent he kept a "steady Heart" (l. 431), he had to work at it. Patrick Delany observed this tendency in Swift's resolute efforts to discipline his avarice through charitable donations.[5] Some of the eulogist's statements, then, more nearly express hopes or intentions than facts, Swift understandably being more aware of his efforts than of their results. He tells us that "He never thought an Honour done him,/ Because a Duke was proud to own him," and that "He never courted Men in Station,/*Nor Persons had in Admiration*" (ll. 319-20, 325-26). Of course Swift enjoys the attention of the noble and powerful; if I am correct, he is aware that he enjoys it and guards against enjoying it too much. He wishes to clarify his motives, to assure himself and any who may doubt him that he is not obligated to a duke who notices him: Swift wishes to establish himself in the position of condescension even to dukes. This posture, often evident in the eulogy, has

Even in this more complex and persuasive analysis, the essential claim remains, and Swift repeats it elsewhere.[8] The picture corresponds in general to the facts of Swift's patronage as he understood them at the time; and a doubtful case or two—the patronage of an occasional cousin-in-law—would not alter the broad outline. The story recurs, probably because it is one of the clearest and most public facts Swift can use to support his claim that he is a man of principle, who has not sacrificed the public good or his personal friendships to gain wealth or power.

The conflict between the panegyrical persona and Swift's efforts at a more circumstantial self-presentation is clear enough in the following passage, in which the first-person pronoun seems to fit Swift's point of view but not necessarily the eulogist's:[9]

> "And, oh! how short are human Schemes!
> "Here ended all our golden Dreams.
> "What St. John's Skill in State Affairs,
> "What Ormond's *Valour,* Oxford's Cares,
> "To save their sinking Country lent,
> "Was all destroy'd by one Event.
> "Too soon that precious Life was ended,
> "On which alone, our Weal depended.
>   (ll. 371-78)

It has been objected that these lines do not represent Swift's true feelings about Queen Anne or the Tory ministry.[10] But the passage functions rhetorically as part of a contrast between Anne's reign and that of George I, in which Swift satirizes the dire effects of the "faction" in power since the queen's death, and therefore heightens the account of her ministry. The queen herself is brought in merely as a symbol of that ministry. She appears here as she does in this account Swift writes in 1736: "I have seen since the Death of the late Queen (who had few equals before her in every Virtue, since

Monarchy began) so great a Contempt of Religion, Morality, Liberty, Learning, and common Sense, among us in this Kingdom; a hundred Degrees beyond what I ever met with in any Writer antient or modern." Similarly, writing in 1738, Swift underscores the desirability of "a defence of [the Tory] Ministry, and a justification of our late glorious Queen, against the malice, ignorance, falsehood, and stupidity of our present times and managers."[11] Moreover, Anne's life was literally "precious," in that "our Weal" did literally "depend" on it. Upon her death, the Tories were out: "how short are human Schemes!"

The footnotes support the eulogy in a series of more nearly factual and circumstantial accounts. The reliability of their information about Swift has also been underestimated. One case in point is the claim that in 1727, Caroline "being then Queen, the Dean was promised a Settlement in England" (l. 184n.). Murry flatly denies that that occurred, but at the time Swift pretty clearly thought that he had been offered such a settlement.[12] Indeed, although the matter was ambiguous, his understanding may well have been correct. We see here, as in the "Verses" as a whole, Swift's urge to clarify.

A different case is Swift's note to line 435: "In *Ireland* the Dean was not acquainted with one single Lord Spiritual or Temporal. He only conversed with private Gentlemen of the Clergy or Laity, and but a small Number of either." This note has been described as "hyperbole . . . so gross that it has the effect of a lie."[13] Yet the effect very nearly vanishes when we recall Swift's stipulation that "this Poem still preserves the Scene and Time it was writ in" (l. 189n.). Swift's contact with the Dublin court seems to have ended when Carteret left in the spring of 1730. From then onward for many months— that is, during the composition of the "Verses"—Swift boasts about his lack of lordly acquaintance.[14] *Acquaintance* can of course be applied inclusively or exclusively; Swift makes clear his exclusive meaning at this time in a letter to John Winder:

"There is not one spirituall or temporal Lord in Ireland whom I visit, or by whom I am visited." That is, he is not on calling terms with any of these men. He tells Pope, "I am not acquainted with one Lord either Temporal or Spiritual, nor with three Squires, a half dozen middling Clergymen are all the Croneys I have." To Knightley Chetwode he writes, "I thank God that I am not acquainted with one person of title in this whole kingdom, nor could I tell how to behave myself before persons of such sublime quality. Half a dozen middling clergymen, and one or two middling laymen make up the whole circle of my acquaintance."[15] Chetwode in his joshing reply identifies the context that surely excited Swift's repetition of this topic: the complaints of Lord Allen ("Traulus") against Swift's "A Libel on Dr. Delany" in the Irish Privy Council and House of Lords early in 1730. In these accusations Allen was a blatantly false friend, as Swift took care to point out in a public denunciation: Allen "had, for several years, caressed and courted, and solicited his [Swift's] friendship more than any man in either kingdom had ever done; by inviting him to his house in town and country, by coming to the Deanry often, and calling or sending almost every day when the Dean was sick, with many other particulars of the same nature, which continued even to a day or two of the time when the said person made those invectives in the Council and House of Lords."[16] Thus Lord Allen fits perfectly the satiric pattern of the "Verses," in which Swift refers over and over to the personal obligations of friendship and gratitude.

The assertion that Swift had no social friendships with members of the Irish House of Lords at the time he wrote the "Verses" is, so far as I can tell, correct. By dwelling on it, Swift argues both that he is not getting the acclaim he deserves, and that his not associating with such people is to his credit: more hyperbolically, "He would have held it a Disgrace, / If such a Wretch had known his Face" (ll. 441-42).

The reader is meant to contrast the mock-nobility of Ireland with the more powerful and estimable English princes and noblemen mentioned earlier in the poem.

Most other statements in the eulogy could be similarly annotated. In summary, the eulogy as a whole is far closer to a serious representation of Swift than is sometimes supposed. It offers recognition he thought he deserved (though probably not *all* the recognition he thought he deserved), and it permits him the convenience of focusing on the main currents and characteristics of his public life without accounting for exceptions. Some of the eulogy appears conventional, and whether Swift thought of these passages as *merely* conventional may be hard to tell. I see no entirely satisfactory way to explain the remark that Swift "lash'd the Vice but spar'd the Name" (l. 460), even though it might be argued, I think, that Swift's name-sparing efforts in his published writings up to this time had been extensive. Such a line may result from an unresolved conflict between, on the one hand, Swift's intention to distance himself from the eulogy (whether by ironic humor, or by making the eulogist ill-informed, selfish, or conventional in his compliments), and, on the other hand, Swift's intention to present himself straightforwardly and convincingly (most evident in the footnotes and in the eulogy's proximity to opinions and stances recurrent in Swift's letters). But here as in the eulogy generally, Swift is in a militant posture, sometimes attacking and sometimes defending, but always asserting his honor and reputation; he is concerned to make a good figure, in an age that believed a gentleman *should* make a good figure and that thought heroic actions were possible.[17]

It has been suggested that in the eulogy Swift puts forward a myth about himself.[18] I would add that it is a myth he himself took seriously. He could do so because the myth is made out of the intractable materials of fact, though he would hardly be human if he had not let some self-deception, some lapse of memory, some self-indulgent clarification of ambiguity color the story. The very egoism which loads the story and its footnotes with facts—which needs to define the self as knowledgeable and objective—elicits the distortions of fact. Swift did not invent the myth specifically for "Verses on the Death of Dr. Swift"; rather it grew from remembered occasions and from ordinary and habitual attitudes. We have in the eulogy a good indication of the righteous sense of self-identity from which much of Swift's satire springs; and if he is often humorously self-deprecating, this is the self he deprecates.

Events pattern themselves as motifs in Swift's account of himself. He had been well received at court, and that was a token of his merit. He is the victim of false friendship and ingratitude; his recognition, when he gets it, ironically comes from the rabble or from one as insignificant as the eulogist. He is a man of principled integrity; his exile results from his virtue: " 'Had he but spar'd his Tongue and Pen, / He might have rose like other Men.' " The apparently gratuitous praise of the eulogy seems less so once we consider its contexts, the more recent being the more animating: Swift's loneliness; his continuing fame as Drapier; his fury at Lord Allen; his apparent betrayal by Queen Caroline's false friendship; his resentment at attacks on his integrity—the tales, for instance, of his having bargained with Walpole for a bishopric in 1726; his sense of Ireland as a mock kingdom with a mock parliament; and most significantly, his knowledge that "the Time is not remote, when I / Must by the Course of Nature dye."

NOTES

1. *Literary Meaning and Augustan Values* (Charlottesville: University Press of Virginia, 1974), pp. 33-37.

2. This approach is suggested by Robert W. Uphaus's article, "Swift's 'Whole Character': The Delany Poems and 'Verses on the Death of Dr. Swift,' " *Modern Language Quarterly* 34 (1973): 406-16; see especially pp. 413-14.

3. *The Correspondence of Jonathan Swift*, ed. Sir Harold Williams, rev. David Woolley, 5 vols. (Oxford: Clarendon Press, 1963-1972), 1:262; 4:230. Hereafter cited as *Corr.*

4. *The History of the Four Last Years of the Queen*, in *The Prose Writings of Jonathan Swift*, ed. Herbert Davis, 14 vols. (Oxford: Blackwell, 1939-68), 7: xxxiv-xxxv. This edition is hereafter cited as *Prose.*

5. [Patrick Delany], *Observations upon Lord Orrery's Remarks* (London: Reeve, 1754), pp. 12-13, 259-60.

6. *Corr.*, 1: 330.

7. Herbert Davis, "Swift's Character," in *Jonathan Swift 1667-1967: A Dublin Tercentenary Tribute,* ed. Roger McHugh and Philip Edwards (Dublin: Dolmen Press, 1967), p. 11.

8. *Corr.*, 2: 370; 4: 98-99; 2: 445; see also *Corr.*, 3: 419-20; 4: 556; *Four Last Years, Prose,* 7: xxxv; *An Enquiry into the Behaviour of the Queen's Last Ministry, Prose,* 8: 131.

9. For an interesting effort to account for this apparent difficulty, see Peter J. Schakel, "The Politics of Opposition in 'Verses on the Death of Dr. Swift,' " *Modern Language Quarterly* 35 (1974): 246-56.

10. Arthur H. Scouten and Robert Hume, "Pope and Swift: Text and Interpretation of Swift's Verses on His Death," *Philological Quarterly* 52 (1973): 227-28.

11. *Corr.*, 4: 488n.; 5: 117; see also Swift's will, *Prose,* 13: 154.

12. John Middleton Murry, *Jonathan Swift: A Critical Biography* (London: J. Cape, 1954), pp. 410-13. I have examined this point in detail in "Friends and Enemies in *Verses on the Death of Dr. Swift,*" in *Studies in Eighteenth-Century Culture,* vol. 8 (Madison, Wis.: University of Wisconsin Press, 1979), pp. 205-32.

13. Ehrenpreis, *Literary Meaning,* p. 35.

14. This posture of being cut off from the nobility is one Swift seems to have relished; it occurs occasionally in earlier letters he sent to England, though not with the repeated insistence found during the period when "Verses" was being composed. See *Corr.*, 2: 302; 3: 289.

15. *Corr.*, 4: 4; 3: 396, 462; see further "Considerations about Maintaining the Poor," *Prose,* 13: 175.

16. "The Substance of What Was Said by the Dean," *Prose,* 12: 145-46.

17. See "Of Mean and Great Figures Made by Several Persons," *Prose,* 5: 83-86.

18. David M. Vieth, "The Mystery of Personal Identity: Swift's Verses on His Own Death," in *The Author in His Work: Essays on a Problem in Criticism,* ed. Louis L. Martz and Aubrey Williams (New Haven, Conn.: Yale University Press, 1978), p. 254.

10

Imagination and Satiric Mimesis in Swift's Poetry:
An Exploratory Discussion

DONALD C. MELL, JR.

University of Delaware

Writing on Swift's verse has, in the past decade, become a major critical industry, the new wave, so to speak, of Augustan literary interests—surely an ironic response to Samuel Johnson's observation: "In the Poetical Works . . . there is not much upon which the critick can exercise his powers."[1] Because of this activity, our appreciation and understanding of Swift has been immeasurably enhanced. We now know more about the poet behind the many masks and masquerades, about biographical matters and circumstances of publication, about his parodic and burlesque techniques, about the moral norms (or lack of them) informing his structures, about his use not only of the style and manner of the revered Horace and Virgil, but also about his adaptations of the practices and traditions of his Medieval, Renaissance, and seventeenth-century predecessors.

123

This vigorous and sustained interest in Swift's poetry has not, however, dispelled doubt about his full commitment to the Augustan ideal of the poetic imagination as an instrument for transforming the particulars of experience and shaping them into moral and aesthetic order, about his faith in the mimetic function of art; indeed, Martin Battestin, who devotes his book *The Providence of Wit* to the very proposition that Augustan art manifests the idea of order in metaphysical, moral, and aesthetic realms, describes Swift as "ridiculing the pride and pretensions of men and mocking the forms—especially the poetic forms—which dignified them."[2] This anti-poetic view of Swift has a long history, and some of the most respected scholars of the period have promoted it. Ricardo Quintana has spoken of the "unique" quality of "Swift's uncompromisingly hostile view of the poetic imagination" and has called the two description poems "Morning" and "City Shower" examples of anti-poetic realism. Herbert Davis uses more sweeping terms, calling Swift "the most extreme example" in England of reaction against the romantic and heroic view of the poet's function and art. More damaging, at least given the thesis of this paper, is Oswald Johnston's contention that, unlike Pope, who has "full confidence in the capacity of serious poetic forms—of poetic language—to express all that he needs to express," Swift "does not allow us to settle upon a recognizable poetic style as means of judgment—as a fixed standard whose values we share and against which we can measure divergences." Perhaps the most radical indictment of Swift's faith in the ability of language to sharpen experience into moral and poetic value is A. B. England's assertion that the very "randomness" of Swift's rhetoric—the crazy rhymes, the loose structure, the unpredictable changes in tone—"gives the impression of mimicking . . . the disordered state of that actuality which it describes."[3]

These characterizations of Swift as an anti-poetic realist and the reductionist view of his art as an undifferentiating mirror of actuality may attest, as much as anything else, to the pervasiveness of F. R. Leavis's famous depiction of his prose "intensities" as those of "rejection and negation."[4] But Swift's own pronouncements on language and style sometimes seem uncomfortably close to that anti-aesthetic distrust of the imagination made fashionable by Locke and other Restoration theorists of language,[5] and there are many specific references in the poems to this aspect of Swift's poetic consciousness. For example, in an early poem "Occasioned by Sir William Temple's Late Illness and Recovery" (1693), Swift simply renounces the Muse:

> There thy enchantment broke, and from this hour
> I here renounce thy visionary pow'r;
> And since thy essence on my breath depends,
> Thus with a puff the whole delusion ends.[6]
>   (ll. 151-54)

Later, to Lady Acheson, Swift insists on the need to "Talk with Sense" in order to "Learn to relish *Truth* and *Reason*." Drawing on a familiar Augustan metaphor of comic disappointment,[7] he equates the use of heroic or sublime poetic style with the flight of a rocket that rises, burns out, and falls to earth—a mere sport or humorous spectacle of no moral significance:

> Shou'd I attempt to climb,
> Treat you in a Stile sublime,
> Such a Rocket is my Muse,
> Shou'd I lofty Numbers chuse,
> E'er I reach'd *Parnassus* Top
> I shou'd burst, and bursting drop.
>   ("An Epistle to a Lady," ll. 257-62)

And to Patrick Delany, friend and confidant, he writes in 1718:

> To you the Muse this Verse bestows,
> Which might as well have been in Prose;
> No Thought, no Fancy, no Sublime,
> But simple Topicks told in Rime.
> ("To Mr. Delany," ll. 9-12)

Important as such passages are (and there are numerous others in the same vein) in assessing Swift's overall attitude toward language and poetic art, such disclaimers are not uncommon in Renaissance or Augustan poetry, and often amount to something of a pose, a stance on the part of the poet. Pope, we recall at the end of "Windsor-Forest," leaves to his friend, the poet George Granville, "The Thoughts of Gods," while his own "humble Muse, in unambitious Strains," concerns itself with the simplicities of the pastoral.[8] In "Epistle II, ii," moreover, where he announces that *"plain* Prose must be my fate," Pope purports to give up entirely the "Rules of Poetry" in order to "learn to smooth and harmonize my Mind," turning from artifice and art to the cultivation of self, ironically, in this case, a notion thoroughly stylized and Horatian. In fact, in "An Epistle to a Lady," just cited, Swift brilliantly turns ostensible blame into sincere compliment by constructing a mock-apology for his inability to write heroic praise at the same time he indirectly idealizes Lady Acheson and denounces the Walpole government in grand, impersonal tones close to the public-defender style of Pope, say, toward the end of "Epilogue to the Satires."

Even Swift's justly famous poems "A Description of the Morning" and "A Description of a City Shower" have a richness and density that belie what appears on the realistic surface. The squalor, both moral and physical, of contemporary urban London is seemingly mirrored directly through unvarnished diction and often crude and insistent rhythms and rhyme. But if the realistic urban scene in "Morning" discredits romanticized and clichéd eighteenth-century versions of a pastoral dawn, the moral disorder of this urban scene is, in turn, satirized through comparison with the authentic classical ideal of pastoral. The admired closing passage of "City Shower" graphically describes the sewerage and filth inevitably washed up in a city after a storm; but the classical precedents of two far more significant storms in Virgil's *Georgics* and *Aeneid* provide a measuring stick to evaluate the contemporary scene.[9] Furthermore, Swift also satirizes the familiar contemporary depictions of these literary storms, especially by imitators like Dryden, through mockery of the stylistic peculiarities of the descriptions such as the use of triplets. The imaginative ideal is not diminished by comparison with the real, nor is the real merely satirized by association with the ideal: both ideal and real comment on and modify one another simultaneously.

Unlike those of Dryden or Pope, Swift's prose and correspondence refer sparingly to the function of the imagination and the nature of art; much less does Swift offer a systematic poetic. Several passages, however, do refer to mimesis in terms beyond those involving the mere reflecting or expressing of an actuality external to the mind. Swift often thought of this process in terms of a conversion or change of something negative into something positive. The Bee in *The Battle of the Books,* we remember, produces honey and wax that is "Sweetness *and* Light," but only as a result of finding its "Livelihood is an universal Plunder upon Nature . . . rob[bing] a Nettle as readily as a Violet," as his scornful adversary, the Spider, accuses him.[10]

Thus the very rejection of false art entails an indirect acknowledging of its opposite—the idealizing imagination. Swift writes in 1730:

> For, though the Muse delights in Fiction
> She ne'er inspires against Conviction.
> ("To *Dr. Delany on the Libels Writ against him,*"
>   ll. 105-6)

And he writes also in "To Stella, Who Collected and Transcribed his Poems" (1720):

> Unjustly Poets we asperse;
> Truth shines the brighter, clad in Verse;
> And all the Fictions they pursue
> Do but insinuate what is true.
>
> (ll. 57-60)

His distrust of imaginative idealization of art is actually not anti-poetic but pro-poetic, and represents an indirect expression of a belief in art's moral force. Swift is not ridiculing poetic language and style because they are irrelevant to man's moral life, but paradoxically because they are in fact the best vehicle for the transmission of virtue and truth, and the only medium through which to present a concept of man and vision of reality. Despite his apparent disparagement at times of poetic inspiration he was, in fact, a self-conscious and committed literary artist; and language, after all, provided the "satyric Touch" for that "Nation want[ing] it so much." Moreover, it became the means of creating a variety of fictional situations and poetic worlds.

Any satirist knows that the power of language and the imagination may distort or obscure the very moral truths he is affirming. The problematic nature of that moral reality forces Swift, as well as his fellow Augustans, into ambiguity and irony, the consequence of a fundamental skepticism colliding with moral idealism. Swift's role as writer is analogous to his favorite rhetorical practice of irony, which allows him to approach truth through indirection and inversion, often saying the opposite of what is meant, but still affirming the truth. An ironist like Swift simultaneously considers many views and attitudes toward his subject matter. But as he executes the satire he acts upon these divergent views with varying degrees of emphasis. This represents Swift's search for self-knowledge, his attempt to create a satiric self, at once skeptical and assured, using irony as an escape hatch but also as an instrument to keep the artistic and moral ideal alive.

Swift's celebrated "On Poetry: A Rapsody" is universally admired by his readers and is representative of his most effective and sustained satire—it is "full of good things," in the words of Ricardo Quintana. More specifically, it has been characterized by Maurice Johnson as Swift's *ars poetica, Essay on Criticism,* and *Dunciad* all rolled up together.[11] An ironically titled satire on George II and the Walpole government, it is, in addition, a good illustration of the complex interplay between the poetic imagination, satire, and politics. Although a political satire, it is also a poem about how politics is perceived and transformed through art. Through the satirical imagination life is converted into art, which in turn reflects life, and such mimetic action emphasizes processes of creation and criticism, satiric method and purpose.

The basic rhetorical strategy of "On Poetry" is one familiar in Swift: it opens, as does "Verses on the Death of Dr. Swift," with sententious moralistic statements about human perversity and pride (ll. 1–24); then, also like "Verses," but without actually employing different spokesmen, the poem proceeds to test and apply the opening moral generalizations by creation of a variety of voices and attitudes in the guise of "an old experienc'd Sinner," purporting to give Imlac-like advice (but without his tolerance or charity) to an aspiring poet. The speaker treats the real difficulties of writing good verse (ll. 25–70); provides his tyro laureate with a list of ironic instructions applicable to either poet or critic (ll. 71–132); attacks contemporary critics' commercialism, false taste, and hack writing (ll. 232–404)—all prominent concerns in Pope's early *Dunciad,* "To Augustus," and *Peri Bathous* of roughly the same period. Finally, Swift composes two abominable court poems parodying the panegyrical style and manner of a Colley Cibber while satirizing George II and Walpole (ll. 405–95).

The four verse paragraphs beginning "Not *Empire* to the rising-Sun" (l. 25) and ending "Gone, where the *Chickens* went before" (l. 70) provide a good instance of Swift's complex attitudes toward poets, poetic imagination, and satiric purpose. I quote the best known and most personal of these passages:

> Not beggar's Brat, on Bulk begot;
> Nor Bastard of a Pedlar *Scot;*
> Nor Boy brought up to cleaning Shoes,
> The Spawn of *Bridewell,* or the Stews;
> Nor Infants dropt, the spurious Pledges
> Of *Gipsies* littering under Hedges,
> Are so disqualified by Fate
> To rise in *Church*, or *Law*, or *State*,
> As he, whom *Phebus* in his Ire
> Hath *blasted* with poetick Fire.
>
> (ll. 33-42)

Here the insistent alliteration and emphatic negation carried by the "Not" and repeated "Nors," the emotional tension generated by syntactic parallelism combine to create effects reminiscent of Pope's righteously indignant response to the character of Sporus in the "Epistle to Dr. Arbuthnot" beginning with the line "Not Fortune's Worshipper, nor Fashion's Fool." In Swift's version, however, the low diction, the tone of bitter self-contempt, the vulgarity and ambivalence of words like "blasted" and "Fire," which suggest both a self-destructive force and genuine creativity, as well as the enthusiasm Swift dreaded—all conspire together in mock outrage that signals his contempt for the Grub Street poet. Also this unfortunate "young Beginner" is illustrative of the perverse ambition and irrational compulsion that drive a poet to attempt success despite the "annual Hundred Pound" and the inevitability of failure. This "Folly" that "fights with *Na-*

ture" (l. 20), the result of that "universal Passion, *Pride*" (l. 3), accounts for the absurdity of such poetic endeavors, illustrated by the if-you-don't-succeed-try-try-again motif behind the "old experienc'd Sinner's" ironical advice to the young poet. The often-noted "*Burlesque* Stile" ("An Epistle to a Lady," l. 50) creates sharply insulting and contemptuous comedy.

But despite the degrading insect and animal imagery that Swift, like Pope in the "Epistle to Dr. Arbuthnot," continually applies to the "rhiming Race," his ridicule is finally not at the expense of all poets and poetry. And the "old experienc'd Sinner," who blames poetic failure on the predicament of Hobbes's "State of War by Nature" is clearly distinct from the true poet who is alienated from and repulsed by contemporary politics and the literary establishment of the 1730s. After all, "To strike the *Muses Lyre*" (l. 32) really does require "heavenly Influence." Thus ambiguous tones of blame and praise, sarcasm and sympathy, contempt and respect, detachment and complicity are necessarily mingled in the wit of the couplet summarizing the sequence:

> Poor starv'ling Bard, how small thy Gains!
> How unproportion'd to thy Pains!
> (ll. 59-60)

Passages in "On Poetry" that actually mimic bad writing and pompous style would appear to support the anti-poetic realist school of critics who argue for a reductionist art in Swift. But the play of ironies in passages like those beginning "Or oft when Epithets you link/ In gaping Lines to fill a Chink" (ll. 167-68), or the more broadly satirical court panegyrics at the poem's conclusion create a further tension between an imaginative ideal and the realities of hack writing. The passage about superfluous poetic filler material has been described by one critic as "loose and undirected," offering no "ordered way toward conclusive definition." The multiplicity of images, ranging from stepping stones, bridges, a cripple's heel support, to the use of dubious illustrations in order to fill gaps on maps, he argues, "takes on a life of its own and makes the question of relationship to a subject seem irrelevant."[12] But the satire in these passages is directed against uninspired and purely mechanical techniques of writing in which inept and inappropriate figures are simply thrown together, a point Swift makes early in the poem by presumably demonstrating this very slackness and inanity while criticizing it:

> And here a *Simile* comes Pat in:
> Tho' *Chickens* take a Month to fatten.
> (ll. 61-62)

The object of ridicule is clear and the method employed not "irrelevant." Critical norms are created internally by means of the deliberately jumbled figures. The difference between Swift's examples and the hack's is precisely his self-conscious artifice, the sense of a controlled aesthetic response missing, as he says, "when Invention fails" and one is reduced to scratching heads and biting fingernails. Slackness is not being imitated by slackness; rather, through a mimetic process, bad verse is being transformed into art.

The mock-panegyrical court poems at the end of "On Poetry" attack Cibber-like failures to master language. The parody involves the juxtaposing of recognizable disparities between an ideal model and the ridiculous laureate version. In this case, as James Tyne has effectively shown, resonances from actual Horatian and Virgilian passages praising the Roman Augustus produce "unsuspected complexity and density,"[13] and the outside standard often missing in Swift. "To prostitute the Muse's Name" in false flattery represents a form of artistic and cultural degeneracy, a situation also lamented in Pope's *Dunciad* and ironically affirmed in the passage reverently glorifying the Grub Street past:

> Yet *thou* hast greater Cause to be
> Asham'd of them, than they of thee.
> Degenerate from their ancient Brood
> Since first the Court allow'd them Food.
> (ll. 363-66)

The present cultural scene represents for Swift a falling off from the imaginative ideal affirmed, for example, in Pope's vision of a triumphant literary past at the end of the first part of his *Essay on Criticism,* a past to be perpetuated in the poetic excellencies of "the meanest of your Sons," or his notion of poetry, in "Epilogue to the Satires II," as the "Heav'n-directed" satirist's "sacred Weapon" finding its target in debased court poetry. Such an ideal in Swift is hinted at in the Virgilian and Horatian echoes, as has been suggested. As with the poetic effect experienced in the passages that mimic poor writing, a standard of judgment is also created by the poem's rhetorical procedures. Like the Beggar Poet at the end of Gay's opera, who sells out to society's values and ends the play happily, Swift appears to end his poem by bringing literature into line with the realities and necessities of English politics. Actually, through the poem's ultimate self-destruction, having it fall under the weight of false praise in a flourish of dashes, lines, asterisks, and omissions, Swift demonstrates the power of genuine art to move and persuade, while underscoring the imaginative ideal totally lacking in the flatteries of court poetry. Like Gay, who both creates and saves his Peachum or Macheath (Walpole) through the power of art, Swift simultaneously creates and destroys his poem, and, paradoxically, through this creative destruction asserts art's triumph over English politics. The nonending reminds us once again of the contrived nature of a verbal construct, a clear sign of the poetic manipulator who regards his verse not as realistic observation but as artificial mode. At the same time it reminds us of the sense in which satiric poetry can communicate moral and aesthetic values despite its fictionality, vulnerability, even absurdity.

In a complicated process of satiric self-definition, Swift moves his readers through a series of idealizations and realizations that challenge expectations about what to praise or blame. By so doing, he demonstrates an awareness of the capacities and limits of the satiric imagination to render moral truths and aesthetic ideals.

NOTES

1. *Lives of the English Poets*, ed. George Birkbeck Hill (Oxford: Clarendon Press, 1905), 3: 65.

2. *Aspects of Form in Augustan Literature and the Arts* (Oxford: Clarendon Press, 1974), p. 216.

3. *The Mind and Art of Jonathan Swift* (New York: Oxford University Press, 1936), p. 276; also *Swift: An Introduction* (London: Oxford University Press, 1962), p. 93; "Swift's View of Poetry" in *Jonathan Swift: Essays on his Satire and Other Studies* (New York: Oxford University Press, 1964), p. 163; "Swift and the Common Reader," in *In Defense of Reading: A Reader's Approach to Literary Criticism*, ed. Reuben A. Brower and Richard Poirier (New York: E. P. Dutton, 1962), pp. 179, 178; *Byron's "Don Juan" and Eighteenth-Century Literature: A Study of Some Rhetorical Continuities and Discontinuities* (Lewisburg, Pa.: Bucknell University Press, 1975), p. 126.

4. "The Irony of Swift," in *Swift: A Collection of Critical Essays*, ed. Ernest Tuveson (Englewood Cliffs, N.J.: Prentice-Hall, 1964), p. 21.

5. See especially *Tatler No. 230, Letter to a Young Gentleman, Lately Entered into Holy Orders*, "Publisher to the Reader" and, of course, the comic treatment of attempts to devise a language useful for dissemination of scientific truths in *Gulliver's Travels*, bk. 3, chap. 5.

6. All quotations are from *The Poems of Jonathan Swift*, ed. Sir Harold Williams, 3 vols., 2d ed. (Oxford: Clarendon Press, 1958).

7. See Paul Fussell, *Samuel Johnson and the Life of Writing* (New York: Harcourt Brace Jovanovich, 1971), p. 229.

8. *Poems of Alexander Pope*, ed. John Butt (New Haven, Conn.: Yale University Press, 1963). All quotations are from this one-volume Twickenham Edition.

9. See Brendan O Hehir, "Meaning in Swift's 'Description of a City Shower,' " *English Literary History* 27 (1960): 194-207.

10. *A Tale of a Tub, To which is added the Battle of the Books and the Mechanical Operation of the Spirit,* ed. A. C. Guthkelch and D. Nichol Smith, 2d ed. (Oxford: Clarendon Press, 1958), p. 231; see also Charles Scruggs, " 'Sweetness and Light': the Basis of Swift's Views on Art and Criticism," *Tennessee Studies in Literature* 18 (1973): 93-104.

11. *Swift: An Introduction,* p. 180; *The Sin of Wit: Jonathan Swift as a Poet* (Syracuse, N.Y.: Syracuse University Press, 1950), p. 15.

12. England, *Byron's "Don Juan and Eighteenth-Century Literature,"* pp. 132-33.

13. "Swift's Mock Panegyrics in 'On Poetry: A Rapsody,' " *Papers on Language and Literature* 10 (1974): 282.

11

Swift's Remedy for Love: The "Scatological" Poems

PETER J. SCHAKEL

Hope College

A decade and a half after "Cadenus and Vanessa," ten years after the "Progress" poems, several years after the poems to Stella, and about the same time as the poems on Lady Acheson, Swift wrote yet another series of poems about women. He never refers to them in his letters or says elsewhere why he wrote them or what he intended by them. A clue is provided, however, by an allusion on the title page of *A Beautiful Young Nymph Going to Bed. Written for the Honour of the Fair Sex. . . . To which are added, Strephon and Chloe. And Cassinus and Peter,* a quarto pamphlet published by J. Roberts in 1734. Below the first title Swift added, *"Pars minima est ipsa Puella sui.* Ovid Remed. Amoris."[1] The epigraph suggests that Swift set out to write his own remedies for love, for the erotic, romantic love attacked in the "Progress" poems and disparaged in the poems to Stella. His "remedies" were to be, like Ovid's, comic poems, with an underlying seriousness. Unlike Ovid, however, Swift could not maintain a light, dispassionate attitude toward his subject matter. As a result, the tones and themes of the "scatological" poems are not sharply defined and they are less effective, both in their comic and serious dimensions, than the earlier poems about women.

The line quoted in the epigraph, "a woman is the least part of herself," is aimed specifically at "A Beautiful Young Nymph," but its context applies more directly to "The Lady's Dressing Room" (1730), in which Strephon is turned into a total misogynist by closely surveying the contents of and implements in Celia's dressing chamber, and by his discovery, in particular, of the unemptied "Chest." Ovid gives, as his ultimate remedy for passion, the following prescription:

> When she is painting her cheeks with concoctions of dyes, go (let not shame hinder you) and see your mistress' face. Boxes you will find, and a thousand colours, and juices that melt and drip into her warm bosom. Such drugs smell of your table, Phineus; not once only has my stomach grown queasy at them.[2] (ll. 351-56)

The passage has obvious affinities to that in which Strephon surveys the litter after Celia, "Array'd in Lace, Brocades and Tissues," issues forth for what is left of the day:

> Here Gallypots and Vials plac'd,
> Some fill'd with Washes, some with Paste,
> Some with Pomatum, Paints and Slops,
> And Ointments good for scabby Chops.
> Hard by a filthy Bason stands,
> Fowl'd with the Scouring of her Hands;
> The Bason takes whatever comes
> The Scrapings of her Teeth and Gums. . . .
> But oh! it turn'd poor *Strephon's* Bowels,
> When he beheld and smelt the Towels.[3]
>
> (ll. 33-40, 43-44)

Ovid's prescription, intended to temper a passion for a specific woman, was not designed to have the general effect this experience has on Strephon, whose "foul Imagination" henceforth "links/Each Dame he sees with all her Stinks:/ And, if unsav'ry Odours fly,/Conceives a Lady standing by" (ll. 121-24).

Swift surely meant the scene this poem presents as comic, with its discrepancies between Celia's orderly appearance when she leaves the room and the confusion she leaves behind, and between Strephon's naive adoration of the sex before his inventory and his disillusioned misogyny after. Other parts of the poem contribute to the comedy, particularly the analogies and allusions used in describing "the Chest" (l. 70):

> As from within *Pandora's* Box,
> When *Epimetheus* op'd the Locks,
> A sudden universal Crew
> Of humane Evils upwards flew;
> He still was comforted to find
> That *Hope* at last remain'd behind;
> So *Strephon* lifting up the Lid,
> To view what in the Chest was hid.
> The Vapours flew from out the Vent,
> But *Strephon* cautious never meant
> The Bottom of the Pan to grope,
> And fowl his Hands in Search of *Hope.*
> O never may such vile Machine
> Be once in *Celia's* Chamber seen!
> O may she better learn to keep
> "Those Secrets of the hoary deep!
>   (ll. 83-98)

Here is Swift the storyteller at his best, pacing the account skillfully, building up carefully to the punch lines in 94 and 98, and using allusions to increase the wit and satire. Not only do the allusions put excretion in proper perspective—by contrast to the enormous evils released by Epimetheus or Pandora and by Sin—but they also extend the limits of the "remedy." The Pandora legend, from its earliest available account in Hesiod, stands as a warning against woman as a snare, a punishment, the source of the evils in the world:

> Forthwith the famous Lame God moulded clay in the likeness of a modest maid, as the son of Cronos purposed. . . . And Pallas Athene bedecked her form with all manner of finery. Also the Guide, the Slayer of Argus, contrived within her lies and crafty words and a deceitful nature. . . . And [Zeus] called this woman Pandora [the All-endowed], because all they who dwelt on Olympus gave each a gift, a plague to men who eat bread.[4]

And the allusion to *Paradise Lost* brings in the duplicity of women, as Satan's daughter, Sin, unlocks the Adamantine Gates, opening to view "The secrets of the hoarie deep" (2. 891),[5] and releases sin and death from their confinement. In each case the outrageousness of Swift's application renders the potentially serious allusion comic. And in each case the allusion provides a witty anticipation of Strephon's fate, for in the end he has no hope for good in women and is able to see only chaos and anarchy (*PL* 2. 895-96) in them, refusing to see or credit the "order" behind.

But the poem as a whole is not successful comedy, mostly because Swift was unable to disassociate himself from his material sufficiently. The sounds, as well as the sights, in the first half of the poem convey a harshness that is not at all dispassionate. Listen, for example, to these lines: "Allum Flower to stop the Steams,/Exhal'd from sour unsavoury Streams" (ll. 27-28); "For here she spits, and here she spues" (l. 42); "Begumm'd, bematter'd, and beslim'd" (l. 45). The choice and arrangement of words and sounds are, of course,

Swift's, and their effects are too harsh to allow them to be comic. A similar uncertainty of effect obtains from the cooking analogy:

> As Mutton Cutlets, Prime of Meat,
> Which tho' with Art you salt and beat,
> As Laws of Cookery require,
> And toast them at the clearest Fire;
> If from adown the hopeful Chops
> The Fat upon a Cinder drops. . . .
> (ll. 99-104)

The opening lines are comic, with their ironic comparison of the smells of food and excrement, an association reinforced (perhaps unintentionally) by the phrase "the *hope*ful Chops." As the passage continues, however, the words and sounds become too intense to remain comic:

> To stinking Smoak it turns the Flame
> Pois'ning the Flesh from whence it came;
> And up exhales a greasy Stench,
> For which you curse the careless Wench.
> (ll. 105-8)   (ll. 105-8)

The scene strongly suggests sensations personally offensive to the poet, and the suggestion carries over to the tone of the inventory. Something besides comedy is going on here; deeper feelings of the author are showing through and are working against the comic effects.

Swift's epigraph on the title page links "A Beautiful Young Nymph Going to Bed" with this passage (ll. 341-48) in Ovid's *Remedia Amoris:*

> It will profit, too, of a sudden, when she has not prepared herself for anyone, to speed of a morning to your mistress. We are won by dress; all is concealed by gems and gold; a woman is the least part of herself. . . . Arrive unexpect-

edly: safe yourself, you will catch her unarmed: she will fall, hapless woman, by her own defects.

Swift's poem, generally dated 1731, which follows a prostitute to her rooms and describes in detail her false appearance and real afflictions, is a remedy for lust rather than for love. Ovid disrobes a mistress for the purpose of controlling or limiting, not ending, the passion for her; Swift strips a whore for the apparent purpose of squelching all desire for any such women:

> Then, seated on a three-legg'd Chair,
> Takes off her artificial Hair:
> Now, picking out a Crystal Eye,
> She wipes it clean, and lays it by.
> Her Eye-Brows from a Mouse's Hyde,
> Stuck on with Art on either Side. . . .
> Now dextrously her Plumpers draws,
> That serve to fill her hollow Jaws.
> Untwists a Wire; and from her Gums
> A Set of Teeth completely comes.
> (ll. 9-14, 17-20)

Swift's intent again appears to be comic: what Corinna seems to be and what she is are laughingly contrasted; Corinna certainly is the least part of herself.

What is in reality a sad situation, in the passage quoted above, is made amusing by the wit and lightness with which it is presented. In contrast to "The Lady's Dressing Room," the sounds in the lines often work to keep the reader from taking the scene seriously: "Never did *Covent Garden* boast/So bright a batter'd, strolling Toast" (ll. 3-4); "Pulls out the Rags contriv'd to prop/Her flabby Dugs and down they drop" (ll. 21-22); "And *Puss* had on her Plumpers p-st" (l. 62). A pseudo-pastoral motif enhances the generally comic discrepancies: Corinna is neither "Nymph" (title, l. 65) nor "Goddess" (l. 23); her fourth-floor lodging is no "Bow'r" (l. 8); and, as the poem itself emphasizes, for her "no Shepherd sighs in vain" (l. 2). When Corinna removes her "Crystal Eye" (ll. 11, 61), the poem gives comic concreteness to a metaphor that had praised many a damsel before her:

> Her eye seen in the tears, tears in her eye,
> Both crystals.

> Go, clear thy crystals.[6]

The mock pastoralism introduces a theme of art versus nature that is basic to the passage from Ovid and to all the scatological poems: "But how shall I describe her Arts/To recollect the scatter'd Parts?" (ll. 67-68).

Despite the successful comic elements and the apparent comic intent of the whole, much of the poem is not comic at all. A good many lines invite sympathy for Corinna: "With gentlest Touch, she next explores/Her Shankers, Issues, running Sores" (ll. 29-30). The list of ailments may be intended to cause the reader to be amused, or repulsed, but the reference to "gentlest Touch" wrenches the poem from its light, detached treatment and makes the reader realize that the object with artificial hair, false teeth, and flabby breasts is a human being. In spite of the paradox in the phrase "With Pains of Love," the words following, "tormented lies" (l. 39), as well as the dream, in which she "feels the Lash, and faintly screams" (l. 42), produce a sympathetic response in any sensitive reader and do not fit with the comic elements.

Swift's difficulties in controlling his tone and achieving a unified effect in the poem are best illustrated by the allusion to the *Aeneid* in line 46:

> Or, by a faithless Bully drawn,
> At some Hedge-Tavern lies in Pawn;

Or to *Jamaica* seems transported,
Alone, and by no Planter courted.

(ll. 43-46)

From the first edition, a line on Dido was included as a footnote: "Longam incomitata videtur/ire viam" (she seems to be everwending, companionless, an endless way).[7] The situation is latent with mock-heroic possibilities, as the nightmares of a quean are compared to the visions of a queen. The discrepancy of high versus low, dignified versus debased, is certainly present, but Swift underestimated the effect of having the readers' sympathetic response to Dido carry over to Corinna: in her dream, after all, she, like Dido, is a victim of a man's infidelity. Described objectively, her jilting by a "faithless Bully" could have seemed ironically appropriate, but presented as it is from Corinna's viewpoint, it produces sympathy. The entire analogy of Corinna to Dido is amusing intellectually, but the comedy is undercut by the emotional response. Swift's remedy for lust apparently called for readers to be amused at or repulsed by Corinna: "*Corinna* in the Morning dizen'd,/Who sees, will spew; who smells, be poison'd" (ll. 73-74). For either response, sympathy is fatal, yet sympathy there is.

"Strephon and Chloe," also dated 1731, is an account of and comment on the disillusionment of an ordinary mortal who marries a goddess, only to find, on his wedding night, that she is as human as himself. The Strephon of this poem might have been saved the consequences of his sudden enlightenment if he had had an experience similar to the Strephon of an earlier poem:

O *Strephon,* e'er that fatal Day
When *Chloe* stole your Heart away,
Had you but through a Cranny spy'd
On House of Ease your future Bride,

> In all the Postures of her Face,
> Which Nature gives in such a Case;
> Distortions, Groanings, Strainings, Heavings; . . .
> Your Fancy then had always dwelt
> On what you saw, and what you smelt;
> Would still the same Ideas give ye,
> As when you spy'd her on the Privy.
>
> (ll. 235-41, 245-48)

Though not consistent with the tone of the rest of "Strephon and Chloe," the passage links the poem thematically with the other scatological poems as remedies for love.

The comic intent of the poem is unmistakable and the first 218 lines are good comedy. The story has a fine pace, an even tone, excellent balancing of detail, and an appropriate reversal. There is rollicking farce as well as verbal wit, all built up in a series of ironic juxtapositions. Descriptions of Chloe's goddess-like perfections are set over against deliberate references to the unpleasant characteristics she avoids. Thus, lines 9-10 are paired with 11-12:

> And then, so nice, and so genteel;
> Such Cleanliness from Head to Heel:
> No Humours gross, or frowzy Steams,
> No noisom Whiffs, or sweaty Streams.

References to "Arm-pits," "Dog-Days," and smelly toes form the background against which her irreproachable cleanliness stands out (ll. 22-24).

Such verbal juxtapositionings are mirrored by larger, structural ones, of passage against passage, to show how far from reality Strephon and Chloe really are. The description of the wedding introduces contrasts of the literary with the real, the figurative with the literal, the knowing with the naive.

> Imprimis, at the Temple Porch
> Stood *Hymen* with a flaming Torch. . . .

> The Muses next in Order follow,
> Conducted by their Squire, *Apollo:* . . .
> Behold the Bridegroom and his Bride,
> Walk Hand in Hand, and Side by Side;
> She by the tender Graces drest,
> But, he by *Mars,* in Scarlet Vest.
> (ll. 47-48, 53-54, 57-60)

The couple's awareness of themselves, of each other, and of their new state is as shallow as the allusions to the classical gods and goddesses, listed so properly and conventionally. Enclosing this highly romantic portrait are two passages that contrast to it. The marriage was arranged in a most unromantic fashion; literalization of trite metaphors and verbal irony emphasize the materialism involved:

> But, *Strephon* sigh'd so loud and strong,
> He blew a Settlement along: . . .
> The bashful Nymph no more withstands,
> Because her dear Papa commands.
> (ll. 39-40, 43-44)

The conclusion of the wedding is also marked by the material ("the Parson paid," l. 67) and the physical ("now the Pair must *crown their Joys,*" l. 70). The italicized words epitomize the dichotomy, as the trite euphemism covers over the physical reality. And the speaker's concrete language, as he describes the dilemma facing Strephon after the wedding, contrasts with Strephon's literary abstractness: "But, what if he should lose his Life/By vent'ring *on* his heav'nly Wife" (ll. 103-4). The naive Strephon almost surely is unaware, and the knowing speaker almost as surely is fully aware, of the old double entendre the lines contain.

The juxtapositions of ideal and real extend into the romantic, conventional explanation of Chloe's hesitation in lines 145-60 (e.g., "Resistance on the Wedding-Night/Is what our Maidens claim by Right"). In contrast stands the real explanation, in lines 161-92: "The Bride must either void or burst." The contrast is sustained in the disparity between conventional marriage portraits, with cupids and a pastoral setting (ll. 193-202), and the disillusionment that sets in (ll. 203-18) as Strephon hears "the fuming Rill" (l. 175). Mock-heroic allusions to *Paradise Lost* throughout this section indicate the unimportance of the whole affair and the folly of the couple. The tone is raised to a pseudo-Miltonic level by similes and learned allusions. The woman "falls" first and the man, "Inspir'd with Courage from his Bride" (l. 189), follows her example. The cupids fly away like the guardian angels, and chaotic bickering and strife set in. The comic analogue serves as an implicit comment on the episode, and the poem, to this point, provides a witty synopsis of the petty follies of humankind.

Had the poem ended there, "Strephon and Chloe" would have been a successful, lightly satiric, comic poem. But the final ninety-six lines of heavy-handed sermonizing destroy the unity and, by not letting the situation speak for itself, the effectiveness of the poem. They also expose an apparent inconsistency in Swift's purposes in the scatological poems: he wants to know but not get too near the realities in question. In line 253 Swift calls defecation a "Blemish" which, decency requires, must be hidden. A man must, apparently, be aware that women do have such a "natural Defect" (l. 274), but women must take great care that men are never confronted by it:

> Since Husbands get behind the Scene,
> The Wife should study to be clean;
> Nor give the smallest Room to guess
> The Time when Wants of Nature press.
> (ll. 137-40)

There is no evidence that these lines are ironic or even distanced from Swift. They appear to bring out personal feelings of the author and reveal, despite the frequent use of

scatology in his verse and prose, a certain uneasiness with the
subject. Ovid, further along in *Remedia Amoris,* writes "he
who says o'er much 'I love not' is in love" (l. 648). Perhaps it
is the same with one who says o'er much that excretion does
not bother him. Such an uneasiness leads to the emphasis,
probably greater than is called for, on discreetness in the
poems. The offensive or potentially offensive should not be
ignored, but it should be hidden, kept behind the scenes: "To
him that looks behind the Scene,/*Satira's* but some pocky
Quean" ("The Lady's Dressing Room," ll. 133-34). "*Satira,*"
in the Williams edition, is a misprint for "*Statira,*" which
"contrasts Lee's virtuous queen {in *The Rival Queens*} with
the 'pocky' actress who plays the role."[8] Surely one must not
be so naive that one confuses the character with the actress.
But Swift seems to be asking if one will appreciate the play
any better for having seen the cast before they are made up.
Elsewhere he suggests that one will not:

> Why is a handsome Wife ador'd
> By ev'ry Coxcomb, but her Lord?
> From yonder Puppet-Man inquire,
> Who wisely hides his Wood and Wire.
> ("Strephon and Chloe," ll. 283-86)

Women should, then, keep men "deluded" ("Strephon and
Chloe," l. 143), not "By help of Pencil, Paint and Brush"
("The Progress of Beauty," l. 46), but through the "utmost
Cleanlyness" and the greatest decency ("Verses to Vanessa,"
l. 4).

The contrast, invited by the allusions, between Ovid's
light, dispassionate comedy and the heavier, more intense
tone that invades Swift's, points to the difficulties Swift had
with his subject. Ovid approves of passion generally and
urges those who have delight in their love to "rejoice and sail
on"; neither in theme nor tone does Swift ever convey such
approval. Ovid accepts and uses the physical: satiety with, or
distaste after coition is a principal "remedy" for excess pas-

sion. Swift shows no such tolerance: coition is replaced in his poems by excrement or ugliness, and Swift himself is in some degree offended by what he satirizes his characters for being offended at. Recent criticism has been very valuable in demonstrating that Swift was neither mad nor utterly misanthropic in the scatological poems; but it has created a new misunderstanding by assuming that Swift was in total control of his feelings and art, using scatology skillfully as a satiric or moralistic weapon. The main value of the scatological poems, however, lies not in their handling of theme and style, but in their disclosure of a fallible, uncertain, struggling Swift, trying to work through unwanted feelings, but not succeeding entirely. The scatological poems provide, in an entirely unintended manner, the most intimate glimpse into himself that Swift ever permitted.[9]

NOTES

1. See Herman Teerink, *A Bibliography of the Writings of Jonathan Swift*, 2d ed., rev. by A. H. Scouten (Philadelphia: University of Pennsylvania Press, 1963), p. 363. For a different reading of the allusion, see Felicity Nussbaum, "Juvenal, Swift, and *The Folly of Love*," *Eighteenth-Century Studies* 9 (1976): 540-52.

2. All quotations from the *Remedia Amoris* are from Ovid, *The Art of Love, and Other Poems*, trans. J. H. Mozley, Loeb Classical Library, rev. ed. (London: Heinemann, 1939).

3. All quotations of Swift's poetry are from *The Poems of Jonathan Swift*, ed. Sir Harold Williams, 3 vols., 2d ed. (Oxford: Clarendon Press, 1958).

4. "Works and Days," ll. 70-82, *The Homeric Hymns and Homerica*, trans. Hugh G. Evelyn-White, Loeb Classical Library, rev. ed. (London: Heinemann, 1936).

5. All references to *Paradise Lost* are taken from *The Student's Milton*, ed. Frank Allen Patterson, rev. ed. (New York: Appleton, Century, Crofts, 1933).

6. "Venus and Adonis," ll. 962-63, and *Henry V*, 2. 3. 54, *The Riverside Shakespeare*, ed. G. Blakemore Evans (Boston: Houghton Mifflin, 1974).

7. *Aeneid* 4. 467-68, *Virgil*, trans. H. Rushton Fairclough, Loeb Classical Library, 2 vols., rev. ed. (London: Heinemann, 1932).

8. David M. Vieth, *Notes and Queries* 220 (1975); 562-63.

9. For an expanded version of this paper see Peter J. Schakel, *The Poetry of Jonathan Swift: Allusion and the Development of a Poetic Style* (Madison: University of Wisconsin Press, 1978), pp. 106-20.

12

Swift and the "agreeable young Lady, but extremely lean"

NORA CROW JAFFE
Smith College

Wishing to praise "Death and Daphne" (1730) in the face of Lord Orrery's indifference, Patrick Delany chooses the "singularity" of the poem as its central feature.[1] *Singular* seems to be just the right word for this poem. In the opening lines Pluto deplores the dearth of dead men since the Peace of Utrecht and insists that the "Old Batchelor" (l. 12) Death seek a wife and beget young Deathlings to forward his work.[2] A council of underworld coquettes rigs Death out like a beau, with the help of owls, ravens, bats, and snakes; and he goes to take up residence in Warwick Lane, among his fellow physicians. Hearing praise of Daphne, or Lady Acheson, Death approaches her as she sits at cards. Because his skeletal frame pokes through the lawyer's parchment he wears as skin, the "extremely lean" lady (title) falls in love. She shows her wit. He advances to touch her. Finding her hand "as dry and cold as Lead" (l. 95), he becomes frightened and runs away.

What is such a poem really about? Why does Swift choose

to make so much fun of Lady Acheson's thinness, not only here but also in "My Lady's Lamentation and Complaint against the Dean" (1728), in "Lady A--S--N Weary of the Dean" (1728?), in "The Grand Question debated. Whether Hamilton's Bawn should be turned into a Barrack or a Malt-House" (1729), and in "A Panegyrick on the D--N, in the Person of a Lady in the North" (1730)? In the poem itself, why are Death and Pluto distinguished, who are usually considered as one? Why does Swift expend so much effort on the grotesque appearance of the spectral lover? Why does Daphne think that he looks like Adonis? Why should she fall in love simply because they resemble each other? Is she attracted to him because he looks like her, or is she smitten with her own appearance because she looks like him? What is Death afraid of? Why does he run away after touching Daphne? Why, for that matter, is Lady Acheson called "Daphne" rather than "Nancy," as in "My Lady's Lamentation," or "Anne," as in "The Revolution at Market-Hill" (1730)?

The theory that answers most questions for me is that Death is a stand-in for Swift himself and that the poem is about the tutorial relationship he cultivated with Lady Acheson, which was similar to his relationships with Stella and Vanessa. A few historical points are pertinent. The three women were all younger than Swift, with progressively greater intervals between his age and theirs. Stella was fourteen years younger, and Vanessa about twenty years younger. Assuming that Lady Acheson was between the ages of twenty and twenty-five when she married the twenty-seven-year-old Sir Arthur in 1715, she was about twenty-five years younger than Swift. The tutor vied with the father in Swift as he strove to inculcate in all three women a love for walking or riding, a hatred for fops, an impeccable pronunciation in reading aloud, and a comprehensive acquaintance with writers in philosophy, religion, politics, and literature. Each woman presented special problems as a pupil: Lady Acheson, for example, liked to wear high-heeled shoes that impeded her walking. A mark of her ineluctable femininity, her shoes thwarted Swift's plans for her improvement through exercise. In "The Revolution at Market-Hill," he devised a scheme to incapacitate her while he stormed her husband's fortress:

> These gaudy Shoes must *Hannah* place
> Direct before her Lady's Face.
> The Shoes put on; our faithful Portress
> Admits us in, to storm the Fortress;
> While tortur'd Madam bound remains,
> Like *Montezume* in golden Chains:
> Or, like a Cat with Walnuts shod,
> Stumbling at ev'ry Step she trod.
>
> (ll. 67-74)

But sometimes the very same problem would recur, giving rise to the impression that Swift saw the women as much alike. Here he chastises Stella in the verses "To Stella, Who Collected and Transcribed his Poems" (1720):

> Your Spirits kindle to a Flame,
> Mov'd with the lightest Touch of Blame,
> And when a Friend in Kindness tries
> To shew you where your Error lies,
> Conviction does but more incense;
> Perverseness is your whole Defence.
>
> (ll. 87-92)

And here he accuses Lady Acheson in the verses "Daphne" (1730):

> Paradoxes weakly wielding,
> Always conquer'd, never yielding.
> . . . .
> Thick her arguments she lays on,
> And with cavils combats reason:

> Answers in decisive way,
> Never hears what you can say:
> Still her odd perverseness shows
> Chiefly where she nothing knows.
>   (ll. 7-8, 11-16)

Stella may have been more pliable, but even the recalcitrant Lady Acheson bent to the discipline of her teacher. Swift wrote, referring to his first visit to Market Hill, from June 1728 to February 1729, "She was my pupil there, and severely chid when she read wrong."[3] Latest and least known of the "triumfeminate," as Swift would call it, she maintained the tradition that Stella and Vanessa had begun. When he met her, in 1728, Vanessa was dead and Stella had just died. Though the crochets of his age and her actual differences from the others affected his attitude and tone, we might still say that he created Lady Acheson in their image to fulfill his need for a tutorial relationship that offered more than pedagogical satisfaction. Despite the notoriety of "Cadenus and Vanessa" (1713), the poem "Death and Daphne" is a clearer statement of what that relationship meant to him.

The three Galateas looked not only like each other: they looked also like their Pygmalion. When Swift praises Stella's learning in his essay "On the Death of Mrs. Johnson" (1728), he says she read Greek and Roman history, understood the Platonic and Epicurean philosophies and perceived the defects in the latter, could point out all the errors of Hobbes in politics and religion, and possessed a true taste for wit and good sense in both poetry and prose.[4] In other words, her opinions and tastes reflected the leanings of her tutor. Some scholars have even found a resemblance between her handwriting and Swift's.[5] Vanessa is extolled for preferring Greek and Roman virtue to modern foppery, for conversing familiarly of foreign customs, rites, and laws, for appreciating writers like Montaigne, and for learning almost too well the

Swiftian maxim that virtue despises the trappings of piety. Pallas has mistaken her for a male, says Swift in "Cadenus and Vanessa," and endowed her with masculine qualities. Prometheus performs the same service for Hester Johnson in "To Stella, Visiting me in my Sickness" (1720):

> Say, *Stella*, was *Prometheus* blind,
> And forming you, mistook your Kind?
> No: 'Twas for you alone he stole
> The Fire that forms a manly Soul;
> Then to compleat it ev'ry way,
> He molded it with Female Clay.
>
> (ll. 85-90)

Swift is unusually literal in accepting an old pedagogical principle we all know well: students are there to be transformed into wizened little replicas of ourselves. In this respect Lady Acheson proved to be troublesome. With her cards, her vapors, and her high-heeled shoes, she could hardly be taken for a man. Swift occasionally tried to unsex her, as when he wrote, in 1732, "She is an absolute Dublin rake, sits up late, loses her money, and goes to bed sick."[6] But the strain of his frustrated efforts to make her more like himself shows clearly in a poem like "Daphne."

He wanted all three pupils to resemble him. The reasons for this become a little more accessible when we turn from these general points to look at "Death and Daphne":

> And now her Heart with Pleasure jumps,
> She scarce remembers what is Trumps.
> For, such a Shape of Skin and Bone
> Was never seen, except her own.
>
> (ll. 59-62)

It must be the blandest assumption that likeness begets love in all literature, except perhaps for Manfred's notion that Astarte is so incredibly beautiful that she even resembles him. It is Swift's assumption, his habit of mind, that is operating here.

> Charm'd with his Eyes and Chin and Snout,
> Her Pocket-Glass drew slily out;
> And, grew enamour'd with her Phiz,
> As just the Counterpart of his.
>
> (ll. 63-66)

Satisfaction comes in a circle; the lover is attracted to a likeness that confirms his prepossession for himself.

But Swift was sixty-three when he wrote "Death and Daphne." Surely he realized how foolish a figure he would cut as a beau. He would look as grotesque as Death coming to court a young and agreeable lady:

> From her own Head, *Megaera* takes
> A Perriwig of twisted Snakes;
> Which in the nicest Fashion curl'd,
> Like *Toupets* of this upper World;
> (With Flow'r of Sulphur powder'd well,
> That graceful on his Shoulders fell)
> An Adder of the sable Kind,
> In Line direct, hung down behind.
> The Owl, the Raven, and the Bat,
> Club'd for a Feather to his Hat.
>
> (ll. 21-30)

Throughout the Market Hill poems, Swift seems unusually conscious of his appearance. His concern for how he might look to the lady is part of his larger effort to assess her reaction to all aspects of his person and temperament. He seldom speculated in print about Stella's and Vanessa's views of him, but in "My Lady's Lamentation," "Lady A--S--N Weary of the Dean," "A Panegyrick on the D--N," and "An Epistle to a Lady, Who desired the Author to make Verses on Her, in the Heroick Stile" (1733), he actually assumes the lady's voice and point of view to comment on his own severity, on his "Tallow Face," "Beetle-brows," "Eyes of Wall," on his tendency to overstay his welcome, on his shabby gown and dirty band, on his uncontrollable temper, on his doubtful motives for writing satire. When he sees himself through Lady Acheson's eyes, his negative appraisal seems to reflect his fears more than his hopes. By writing lightly of the resentment he anticipated from his pupil, he could allay it, at least in his own mind.

The fears are still present in the unsavory description of Death, as the frightened "Old Batchelor" of the poem makes advances that his real-life counterpart would never have dared. The scene exaggerates the unnatural picture of a sixty-three-year-old man courting a woman very much his junior. It also draws out and distorts other implications of the tutorial relationship peculiar to Swift. An old, celibate scholar and clergyman, with a system of pedagogy that covers such matters as eating and walking, binds to himself, with injunctions that supersede the advice of family and friends, a young and agreeable woman who might be much better suited to other activities. It is Death courting Life in another sense.

Such a courtship, in both senses, is aptly represented by the story of Pluto and Proserpina that Swift weaves into the poem. Proserpina is only a child at play when her dark and ancient uncle kidnaps and rapes her. She is the daughter of fruitfulness and the emblem of life; where she walks, spring is the only season of the year. He is the forbidding god of the underworld, appropriately called "Death" in many versions of the myth. Distinguishing between Pluto and Death enables Swift to tell the same story twice with conciseness. In fact, if Death is his own representative in the poem, he is really telling the same story three times.

These hints seem to be lost on Daphne: "She, as he came into the Room,/Thought him *Adonis* in his Bloom" (ll. 57-58). It is a ridiculous mistake, one that reverses the implications of Pluto's story and the facts of the situation by inverting the categories of old and young, godlike and mortal. It is, however, not very different from the mistake Vanessa has made:

> *Vanessa,* not in Years a Score,
> Dreams of a Gown of forty-four;
> . . . .
> *Cadenus* now no more appears
> Declin'd in Health, advanc'd in Years.
> She fancies Musick in his Tongue,
> Nor further looks, but thinks him young.
> (ll. 524-25, 528-31)

Swift probably felt flattered by this hopeful view of his age. He might even have encouraged it in developing his kind of tutorial relationship. When Vanessa declares herself, after all, Cadenus feels not only disappointment and surprise, but also shame and guilt.

If Swift harbored sexual feelings for his last pupil, the shame and guilt must have been increased by the fact of her marriage. We know very little about that marriage. We know, however, that Lord Orrery marked the word *Daphne* with a red asterisk in an annotated copy of his *Remarks* and wrote on the facing page, "Lady Atchison, wife of Sir Arthur Atchison. Separated from her husband."[7] The accompanying passage relates the story of his introduction to "Daphne" and his presence at a moment of typically Swiftian flirtation: " 'That Lady had rather be a DAPHNE drawn by me, than a SACHARISSA by any other pencil.' "[8] Orrery was witness to the tone of the relationship. Could it be that in choosing to note the fact of Lady Acheson's separation he was partially exonerating Swift from charges that might arise from a reading of the poem?

The paradoxical union of Life and Death, with the immediate goal of procreation and the ultimate goal of annihilation, never takes place within the context of the poem. Death runs from the lady because he finds her touch "dry and cold," a rather peculiar consequence of her thinness that makes her less vital than Death himself. Swift ran from the lady because he found her young, agreeable, and married. He probably feared to find her warm and moist. This reason for the Dean's "not Building at Drapier's Hill" serves us better than the strangely flimsy ones he provides in the poem of that name (1730). In attempting to distance himself from Lady Acheson and shore up the shaky pedagogical relationship, he teased her in a manner less kindly than that he had adopted for Stella. He focused almost exclusively on her figure and taunted her with names like "skinny, boney, snip and lean." Such names, like the curious suggestions that Stella and Vanessa were mistaken for men, denied his attraction and her attractiveness by denying her a sexual identity.[9] The attraction remained, as Swift obliquely testified in "The Grand Question debated," where he invented a quasi-sexual rivalry for her favor between a swashbuckling captain and a daggled scholar. But Swift and his poetic counterparts always lost the lady, by default and design.

Throughout Ovid's *Metamorphoses,* the gods who lose their ladies gain a noble recompense, more glorious but still second best. For example, the hamadryad Syrinx, when pursued by Pan, turns into the sheaf of reeds on which the god plays music. A more pertinent story is, of course, the one about Apollo and Daphne. Deprived of his Daphne, Apollo can still embrace a laurel, seal and sign of all his talents and powers. By accident or intention, Swift has given his final pupil the most comprehensible name. It reminds us of a myth that might serve as model for what Swift was doing when he wrote this poem.

13

Freud, Swift, and Narcissism: A Psychological Reading of "Strephon and Chloe"

THOMAS B. GILMORE, JR.

Georgia State University

Many readers have doubted the wisdom of psychoanalytic criticism of Swift.[1] But even though such criticism usually has a weak basis in insufficient or conjectural biographical data, certain psychological concepts, used judiciously to interpret Swift's poems rather than their author, can help to illuminate them. These concepts may reveal that "Strephon and Chloe" has a greater degree of thematic or didactic integrity than has generally been perceived.[2]

The urinary rouzer that Strephon lets fly in his bride's face on their wedding night is unquestionably the climactic shock of the poem. It may seem almost as shocking as the rouzer itself to maintain that its primary effect is pleasurable; yet Emrys Jones, in accounting for the appeal of Pope's characters in Book 2 of the *Dunciad*, affords support for this contention. Jones notes that the characters behave with the uninhibitedness of infants, and that to enter their world is "to experience a primitive sense of liberation."[3] Pope's childish dunces and Strephon's rouzer violate a sexual taboo, thus freeing the reader of these accounts to return vicariously to a state of polymorphous perversity and to recapture the undifferentiated sexual pleasure of infancy. As Freud and other psychologists have pointed out, coprophilia is among the most important components of this pleasure.[4] The reader's acceptance of the rouzer is probably further enhanced by two realizations: that any form of sexual expression is better for Strephon and Chloe than romantic sterility or Strephon's earlier awe of her; and that the particular form their expression takes is inevitable. In spite of their veneer of culture, Strephon and Chloe are so ignorant as to be sexual infants.

Jones understands, of course, that even as Pope conveys the appeal of the dunces in Book 2, he is judging them adversely. Swift's judgment of Strephon and Chloe, while not simultaneous with their wedding night, follows soon after and is extremely harsh. Nevertheless, Swift's continuation of their story in lines 203-18 of the poem is not only credible but psychologically consistent with the rouzer scene. It is as if Swift is forcing us to do a double take: what had seemed at first glance an innocent if infantile sexuality is exposed in the later passage as a symptom of anal fixation or eroticism resulting from narcissism. If this is a normal state in infancy, Swift shows his disgust with it and its manifestations when it completely determines the character of the relationship between two immature adults. Obviously, Swift could not have been familiar with the concept of narcissism as a neurosis (or with the other psychological concepts used in this paper); but especially in his portrayal of Strephon he seems to have exposed that neurosis which current critics like Christopher Lasch and Richard Sennett have begun to regard as a major psychological ill of late twentieth-century American society.[5]

Although Strephon lacks the development or complexity to

be seen as a victim of full-blown narcissism, he possesses several of its most striking features. Even the Strephon of "The Lady's Dressing Room" is a Narcissus figure: the legendary pool into which Narcissus gazes, self-infatuated, becomes Celia's magnifying glass. Strephon is "frighted" (l. 61), not only by its enlargement of his visage but, more important, by the fact that his discoveries about Celia in her dressing room, monstrously magnified as if by her glass, threaten his narcissistic self-love, Celia being for him nothing more than a projection and desired confirmation of his idealized self. His namesake in "Strephon and Chloe" may be less obviously a descendant of Narcissus, partly because he goes through the social rituals of courtship and matrimony. But as his wedding night approaches, Strephon does not look forward to it with desire. The absence of any thought of giving pleasure to Chloe or sharing it with her seems attributable to something other than the understandable nervousness of the sexually inexperienced Strephon. As Richard Sennett observes, "Narcissistic feelings often focus themselves on obsessive questions of whether I am good enough, whether I am adequate, and the like."[6] These are just the sorts of questions running through Strephon's head, especially in lines 71-94. Whatever he may think, he is not in love with Chloe except in a narcissistic way; in his worries about how she will receive his sexual advances, we are able to see that his overriding concern is with using her, as an idealized extension of himself, to affirm or validate a faltering self-image.

Freud wrote of the narcissist that he often chooses to love a person with "excellences which he never had" and cannot attain.[7] One predictable outcome of this hope that someone else can supply inner deficiencies is a disappointment that leaves the narcissist feeling empty or dead.[8] This is exactly the state of Swift's Cassinus (in "Cassinus and Peter"), who not only feels dead but longs for death as a result of his dreadful discovery that Caelia, lovely Caelia, s--ts. But the passivity or resignation of Cassinus is only one type of narcissistic reaction to disillusionment in love, to the profound if usually unconscious "conviction that other people . . . will never be good enough."[9] There is often a further reaction, exemplified by Strephon in both "The Lady's Dressing Room" and "Strephon and Chloe," which can be characterized as a desire for revenge. Vacillating "between the extremes of overidealization and devaluation," narcissists may come "to depreciate and treat with contempt those from whom they do not expect anything (often their former idols)."[10] In "The Lady's Dressing Room," Strephon, having discovered the nastiness of his beloved Celia, generalizes his contempt for her to reach the conclusion that all women stink (ll. 121-28). His namesake in "Strephon and Chloe" obtains his revenge and degrades his beloved by joining with her in a "great Society in Stinking" (l. 210): not really a society at all, of course, but a kind of narcissism *à deux,* a form of sexual perversion "involving primitive aggressive manifestations or primitive replacement of genital aims by eliminatory ones."[11] The perversion also effectively fulfills Strephon's narcissistic desire to block the development of any genuine "social dimension" in his sexuality.[12]

From another viewpoint the impasse of Strephon and Chloe may be explained as the result of their failure to sublimate, to engage in that process by which the sex drive is diverted into numerous channels whose end product is often called culture or civilization. According to Freud, society or community is the closest synonym to civilization; but the "great Society in Stinking" established by Strephon and Chloe after their wedding night is only the noxious, unsublimated travesty of civilized society. Moreover, later in the poem, in a catalogue of female vices, the woman gossip who gives the impression of "breaking Wind" (l. 282) through her mouth may be another instance of anal fixation—and, if so, another travesty of healthy society.

Decency, a term much stressed in the last hundred lines of the poem, is perhaps Swift's equivalent to sublimation; and its result, disclosed in the poem's final paragraph, is friendship, the chief means, according to Freud, of strengthening "the communal bond" and therefore the indispensable material of society or civilization.[13] For Norman O. Brown, "Swift's ultimate horror" in the scatological poems is that "sublimation—that is to say, all civilized behavior—is a lie and cannot survive confrontation with the truth."[14] "Strephon and Chloe" might seem to support this claim in its at times almost desperate insistence that women conceal their defecatory functions; this is perhaps one quality that Peter Schakel has in mind when he speaks of a "fallible, uncertain, struggling Swift."[15] Nevertheless, the poem may be credited with two major victories: it confronts the horror of anality, and Swift's recommendation of the civilizing virtue of friendship survives it.

One may still be dissatisfied with Swift's exclusive attention to anal fixation and friendship, with his neglect of the joys of mature sexuality. But although Freud is explicit on this subject where Swift is tacit, their attitudes are essentially similar. To explain his observation that there is "something in the nature of the [sex] function itself which denies us full satisfaction," Freud advances a theory that is in line with Swift's implications. When man adopted an upright posture, Freud speculates, he began to develop a repugnance to genital odors and to the excremental odors physiologically inseparable from them that necessarily diminishes his sexual pleasures.[16] If Freud does not deny all possibility of sexual enjoyment, as Swift seems to, he agrees that the more civilized a person becomes, the more he will sacrifice or sublimate his sexual urges in favor of such goals as friendship.

Freud entertained no illusions about the bliss of civilization. Indeed, at least once in his writings he briefly considered the possibility that some or all civilizations are neurotic.[17] He was also aware that the renunciations required by civilization are painfully difficult for most people. Nevertheless, Freud would have regarded skeptically, if not with Swiftian derision, Norman O. Brown's idea that man's best hope is to give up civilization and restore his polymorphous perversity.[18] For Freud, the only alternative to civilization was not polymorphous perversity but the state of nature, in which men are inclined to "satisfy their aggressiveness on . . . [their neighbor], to exploit his capacity for work without compensation, to use him sexually without his consent, to seize his possessions, to humiliate him, to cause him pain, to torture and to kill him."[19] As Lady Macleod once murmured of Dr. Johnson, when he observed that man was inherently no more virtuous than a wolf, "This is worse than Swift."[20] If not worse, Freud's dark vision of man in a state of nature underscores his basic affinities with the greatest Augustan writers. And it suggests why, with them, he defended civilization for all its faults and frailties. If Freud's view of man is no more complete than that of the Augustans and if it tends toward Swift's pessimism about the possibilities of sexual delight, it is at least, like Swift's view, less insulting to man's complexity than the massages of *Playboy* magazine or the dream of Norman O. Brown.

Apart from the controversial Houyhnhnms, the closest Swift ever came to a positive vision or version of civilization was, perhaps, in some of the poems to Stella and in the last paragraph of "Strephon and Chloe." It is helpful to think of this paragraph as an abstract of a relationship more fully fleshed out in the Stella poems. Possibly because of the disenchantment with politics stemming from Swift's involvement in the Tory administration of Oxford and Bolingbroke, his model of civilization is a type of ideal relationship or friendship between a man and a woman. We can of course never fully know the realities of Swift's relationship with Esther Johnson; but through the Stella poems, the ending of

"Strephon and Chloe," and other sources, we do know what Swift thought or wanted it to be. And although we also know that Swift invested much effort in molding or educating Esther to fulfill his ideal of womanhood, we cannot fairly characterize his relationship with her, or with the Stella of the poems, as narcissistic. Whatever selfish gratification he may have derived from witnessing the success of his efforts, his primary satisfaction seems to have come from his helping to shape a woman of grace, probity, and intelligence, qualities that would make her worthy of the regard and friendship of equally estimable women and men. That is to say, Swift sought to form a woman possessing qualities very much like those named in the final paragraph of "Strephon and Chloe." If we look to classical myth for an analogue to Swift in his relations with Esther or Stella, the figure we are most likely to remember is not Narcissus but Pygmalion.

In spite of some real confusion and problems with tone in the last hundred lines of "Strephon and Chloe," Swift firmly regains command in the two closing stanzas and neatly rounds off the poem in lines 307-14 by sharply contrasting a healthy relationship with the sick, burlesque "Society in Stinking" of Strephon and Chloe. Since even in these lines he mentions passion and love (ll. 307, 310), Swift does not wholly ignore the element of physical or sexual attraction in a relationship between men and women. He emphasizes, however, the major drawback of this element—its lack of solidity or durability—as a foundation for any relationship by the dense architectural imagery in his next-to-last paragraph and by his contrast between the short-lived blaze or "Fire" (l. 222) of passional love and the "mutual gentle Fire" (l. 313) of friendship. Thus if a preoccupation with beauty or sexual attraction is likely to collapse into the fulsome society of Strephon and Chloe, the absence from a relationship of those virtues which Swift names near the end of the poem—sense, wit, decency, prudence, and good nature—is even more certain to produce misery and failure. To put Swift's "message" in language familiar to the late twentieth century, he is suggesting not only at the end but throughout the poem that there are better alternatives than a relationship in which either the man or the woman treats the other as a sex object. If we doubt or reject Swift's priorities or values, we perhaps only demonstrate our disinclination to make those civilizing renunciations mentioned by Freud and our readiness to embrace the panaceas, *inter urinas et faeces,* of *Playboy* or Norman O. Brown.

NOTES

1. See "Forum," *PMLA* 91 (1976): 465; also my essay "The Comedy of Swift's Scatological Poems," *PMLA* 91 (1976): 33-43. See also Phyllis Greenacre's *Swift and Carroll: A Psychological Study of Two Lives* (New York: American Universities Press, 1955).

2. John M. Aden, "Those Gaudy Tulips: Swift's 'Unprintables,' " in *Quick Springs of Sense: Studies in the Eighteenth Century,* ed. Larry S. Champion (Athens: University of Georgia Press, 1974), p. 28. Peter Schakel, "Swift's Remedy for Love: The 'Scatological' Poems," *Papers on Language and Literature* 14 (1978): 145, complains that "the final ninety-six lines of heavy-handed sermonizing destroy the unity and, by not letting the situation speak for itself, the effectiveness of the poem"; and in this text, p. 146.

3. "Pope and Dulness," Chatterton Lecture on an English Poet, *Proceedings of the British Academy* 54 (1968): 254. Pope's bookseller Chetwood, engaged in a pissing contest with Curll, suffers a mishap similar to Strephon's:

> A second effort brought but new disgrace,
> For straining more, it flies in his own face;
> Thus the small jett which hasty hands unlock,
> Spirts in the gard'ner's eyes who turns the cock.
> *Dunciad* (A), Twickenham ed., bk. 2, ll. 167-70.

Swift, however, is characteristically more violent; Strephon's rouzer ends a verse paragraph, and its effect is not softened by any comic simile like Pope's in lines 169-70. Instead, the rouzer immediately disperses the frail images of romantic love ("little *Cupids,*" "Expiring Shepherds," "silver Meads," ll. 193, 200-201), preparing the way for the "great Society in Stinking" (l. 210), which succeeds romantic illusion for Strephon and Chloe. All quotations are from *The Poems of Jonathan Swift,* ed. Sir Harold Williams, 3 vols., 2d ed. (Oxford: Clarendon Press, 1958).

4. Sigmund Freud, "The Most Prevalent Form of Degradation in Erotic Life" (1912), in *On Creativity and the Unconscious: Papers on the Psychology of Art, Literature, Love, Religion,* ed. Benjamin Nelson (New York: Harper Torchbooks, 1958), p. 185; and Karl Abraham, "Contributions to the Theory of the Anal Character" (1921), in *Selected Papers of Karl Abraham M.D.,* trans. Douglas Bryan and Alix Strachey (New York: Basic Books, 1960), p. 372.

5. See Lasch, "The Narcissist Society," *New York Review of Books,* 30 September 1976, pp. 5, 8, 10-13, and *Haven in a Heartless World: The Family Besieged* (New York: Basic Books, 1977), in which he claims (p. 156) that "the narcissist, not the authoritarian, is the prevalent personality type" today. Two of Sennett's works are cited below.

6. *The Fall of Public Man* (New York: Knopf, 1977), p. 11.

7. "On Narcissism: An Introduction" (1914), in *The Standard Edition of the Complete Psychological Works of Sigmund Freud,* ed. James Strachey, 34 vols. (London: Hogarth Press, 1957), 14: 101.

8. Richard Sennett, "Destructive Gemeinschaft," *Partisan Review* 43 (1976): 348.

9. *The Fall of Public Man,* p. 335.

10. Otto Kernberg, interviewed by Linda Wolfe, "Why Some People Can't Love," *Psychology Today* 12 (1978): 58; Kernberg, *Borderline Conditions and Pathological Narcissism* (New York: Jason Aronson, 1975), p. 17. I am indebted for these references to my friend James A. Glass. The publication of a lead article on narcissism in a popular journal is probably an indication of the rising interest in this subject in contemporary American society.

11. *Borderline Conditions and Pathological Narcissism,* p. 11. Significantly, this quotation appears in a section headed "Polymorphous Perverse Sexual Trends."

12. *The Fall of Public Man,* p. 8.

13. *Civilization and Its Discontents,* ed. and trans. James Strachey (New York: Norton, 1962), p. 56.

14. *Life Against Death* (Middletown, Conn.: Wesleyan University Press, 1959), p. 188.

15. "Swift's Remedy for Love," *Papers on Language and Literature* 14 (1978): 147, and this text, p. 148.

16. *Civilization and Its Discontents,* pp. 52, 53n. See also Freud's "The Most Prevalent Form of Degradation in Erotic Life," in *On Creativity and the Unconscious,* pp. 185-86.

17. *Civilization and Its Discontents,* p. 91.

18. One expression of Freud's skepticism can be found in *The Future of an Illusion,* trans. W. D. Robson-Scott, The International Psycho-Analytical Library, ed. Ernest Jones (New York: Liveright, 1953), p. 11. Defending civilization against the innate destructive, antisocial tendencies of man, Freud submits that the maintenance of every culture must probably involve "coercion and instinctual renunciation"—including, surely, the renunciation of polymorphous perversity. Although more tactful and cautious than Swift would have been with dreams such as Brown's, Freud still treats them as visions of a "golden age" and doubts that they can be realized.

14

Swift's Irony Reconsidered

ROBERT W. UPHAUS
Michigan State University, East Lansing

> How is it possible to expect that
> Mankind will take *Advice*, when they
> will not so much as take *Warning?*[1]

The main problem discussed in this paper has been raised most acutely by F. R. Leavis in his essay "The Irony of Swift,"[2] which deals primarily with Swift's prose. In this essay Leavis begins by examining the disjunction between Swift's ostensible themes, including the moral content of his writings, and the effects his writings have on readers. This disjunction, if we accept it as such, raises important critical questions not only about the kinds of irony and satire that Swift employs, but about the overall moral purpose of Swift's use of irony and satire. Such questions are hardly a recent invention, as a quotation from one of Pope's letters to Swift establishes:

I have not the courage however to be such a Satyrist as you,

169

but I would be as much, or more, a Philosopher. You call your satires, Libels; I would rather call my satires, Epistles: They will consist more of morality than wit, and grow graver, which you will call duller.[3]

If I read Pope's observations correctly, he is saying that his practice of satire differs from Swift's both in kind and purpose. Swift's satire is courageous, libelous, and witty, which is to say that Swift's satire is aggressive and quite often personal. On the other hand, Pope's satire is philosophical, epistolary, and grave—all of which implies that the appeal of Pope's satire is primarily intellectual. To some extent Pope may be echoing the now hackneyed distinction between Juvenalian and Horatian satire; or, if we want to adopt Edward Rosenheim's useful distinction, we might say that Swift's satire veers toward the "punitive," whereas Pope's satire tends toward the "persuasive."[4] In any event, Leavis, too, is quite aware of such distinctions, but unlike Pope and Rosenheim he extends their essentially *descriptive* distinctions into an *evaluative* model for determining not simply the literary effects, but moral merit, of Swift's writings. Thus Leavis writes:

There are writings of Swift where "critical" is the more obvious word (and where "intellectual" may seem correspondingly apt)—notably, the pamphlets or pamphleteering essays in which the irony is instrumental, directed and limited to a given end. The *Argument Against Abolishing Christianity* and the *Modest Proposal,* for instance, are discussible in the terms in which satire is commonly discussed: as the criticism of vice, folly, or other aberration, by some kind of reference to positive standards. But even here, even in the *Argument,* where Swift's ironic intensity undeniably directs itself to the defense of something that he is intensely concerned to defend, the effect is essentially negative. The positive itself appears only negatively—a kind of skeletal presence, rigid enough, but without life or body; a necessary precondition, as it were, of directed negation. The intensity is purely destructive. (pp. 16-17)

Leavis is here cited in such detail because he has raised the central question of whether Swift's use of irony and satire is "discussible in the terms in which satire is commonly discussed." Clearly, we can discuss Swift's satire, both in his poems and in his prose, as a criticism of vice and folly, but sometimes we cannot do so "by some kind of reference to positive standards." For example, the history of reader responses to *A Tale of a Tub* and *Gulliver's Travels* suggests that Swift certainly vexed the world, but that vexation may itself have been prompted by Swift's inability or unwillingness to sustain a satisfactory "positive standard."[5]

Thus, comparing Gibbon's irony with Swift's, Leavis argues that the "pattern of Gibbonian prose insinuates a solidarity with the reader," whereas "the implied solidarity in Swift is itself ironical—a means to betrayal." Leavis further observes that Gibbon's irony "habituates and reassures," while Swift's is "essentially a matter of surprise and negation; its function is to defeat habit, to intimidate, and to demoralize" (pp. 17-18). The main example that Leavis uses to support the idea that Swift's irony betrays the reader comes from Section 9 of *A Tale of a Tub*, specifically the two famous paragraphs on deception and madness. What Leavis attempts to demonstrate (I think quite persuasively) is that the operative thematic distinction between "curiosity" and "credulity" finally cancels itself out, leaving the reader to his own resources. That is, the reader is initially lured into believing that Swift is attacking "curiosity" in defense of the "common forms" associated with the Church of England and, by implication, with "credulity." This part would accord well with Swift's claim that he wrote the *Tale* to expose "the numerous and gross Corruptions in Learning and Religion." But by the end of the second paragraph, which concludes "This is the sublime and refined Point of Felicity, called, the *Possession of being well-deceived*, The Serene Peaceful State of being a Fool among Knaves,"[6] the alternative, or, if you will, the positive of "credulity" has been thoroughly discredited.[7] Hence the reader is left without a positive model to hold on to, except, as Leavis says, "the actuality of presentment" (p. 28), which is to say the energy of Swift's presence.

Nevertheless, despite Leavis's dissatisfaction with "the actuality of presentment" as a positive, this essay will suggest that Swift's biographical presence in his later poems replaced, even if it does not mediate, the ironic contrasts of his earlier prose works. He, Jonathan Swift, steps into what Leavis views as the thematic choice between curiosity and credulity. As Maurice Johnson has noted, there exists in much of Swift's poetry "the biographical presence that one strongly feels but cannot quite account for,"[8] and this presence points to significant differences between Swift's prose and poetic satires. The missing "positive" that Leavis talks about in *A Tale* is continually present in Swift's poetry, but that positive performs more a personal than a thematic function. That is, in these poems we are continually presented with Swift's estimate of things—with his personal convictions rather than his putative fictions—and we can accept or reject his convictions, but we cannot ignore them. In fact, part of the difficulty in accounting for that biographical presence is that many of us have been trained to follow the critical strictures having to do with the affective and intentional fallacies and the use of *personae,* and while some of these techniques do work on Swift's prose satires, they do not, in the main, seem answerable and responsive to the strongly personal qualities of Swift's later poetry.

Stated another way, Swift's later poems—namely, the poems written after 1726—frequently reveal what his satiric prose more often conceals. I have already argued in another essay that

> we can spend all the time we want trying to sort out the "irony" of the impartial character in "Verses on the Death of Dr. Swift," but I suggest that the very complexity of this

unique character is both the culmination of what began in the Delany poems and, just as importantly, a basically factual representation of how Swift sees himself.[9]

This argument can be carried a step or two further to suggest that we are so conditioned by Swift's use of irony and satire in his prose works that we seek the same rhetorical complexity in much of his poetry when, in fact, that complexity does not exist. Swift's later poetry is especially important because in these poems he overtly discusses his understanding of himself, his art, and his estimate of the public, as well as the public's estimate of him. These poems show a Swift who is no longer interested in irony and satire as much as he is preoccupied with flat-out attack and self-defense; and if these poems are controversial, they are so not because of their puzzling meaning, but because of their blunt explicitness and strident claims.

For example, during the late 1720s and on into the 1730s Swift was fond of likening himself to a freeman among slaves (*Corr.*, 4: 171). We might think that this is the conventional posture of the satirist, but it is not. Rather, it is a conviction that Swift reverts to repeatedly. In the poem "Holyhead. Sept. 25. 1727," he speaks of going "in freedom to my grave,/Than Rule yon Isle and be a Slave" (ll. 33-34).[10] The poem entitled "Ireland" (1727) begins, "Remove me from this land of slaves/Where all are fools, and all are knaves"; and in the remarkable poem "Verses occasioned by the sudden drying up of St. Patrick's Well" (1729?), he identifies himself with St. Patrick—he is, after all, the Dean of St. Patrick's—and writes:

> WRETCHED *Ierne!* with what Grief I see
> The Fatal Changes Time hath made in thee.
> The Christian Rites I introduc'd in vain:

Lo! Infidelity return'd again.
Freedom and Virtue in thy Sons I found,
Who now in Vice and Slavery are drown'd.
(ll. 33-36)

A similar preoccupation with slavery, and by implication with Swift's freedom, appears throughout "Verses on the Death of Dr. Swift" (1731), and one of Swift's last poems, "On a Printer's being sent to Newgate" (1736), begins: "Better we all were in our Graves/Than live in Slavery to Slaves" (ll. 1-2). This is the dominant note of Swift's later poetry, a tone of disgust, frustration, and isolation, where the absence of irony is conspicuous. In these poems Swift does not elaborate a literary theme designed to appeal to the reader's intellectual understanding, so much as he expresses his outrage, which exists in direct relation to his sense of isolation. He persistently sees himself as a person who for liberty "boldly stood alone" ("Verses on the Death of Dr. Swift," l. 349).

Moreover, to read some of these later poems is to read about a man who has replaced poetic artifice with personal animus, and who has substituted a sense of damnation for any attempts at mediation. Although many of these poems do not generally receive critical attention, I would suggest that they are extremely important because they depict a Jonathan Swift who has abandoned any hopes of reforming the evils around him. Indeed, Swift precisely describes the characteristic tone and intention of these poems when he declares in *An Answer to a Paper called a Memorial* (1728):

I have now present before me the Idea of some Persons, (I know not in what Part of the World) who spend every Moment of their Lives, and every Turn of their Thoughts while they are awake, (and probably of their Dreams while they sleep) in the most detestable Actions and Designs; who delight in *Mischief, Scandal,* and *Obloquy,* with the *Hatred* and *Contempt* of all Mankind against them; but

chiefly of those among their own Party, and their own Family such, whose *odious Qualities* rival each other for Perfection: *Avarice, Brutality, Faction, Pride, Malice, Treachery, Noise, Impudence, Dulness, Ignorance, Vanity,* and *Revenge,* contending every Moment for Superiority in their Breasts. Such Creatures are not to be reformed; neither is it Prudence, or Safety to attempt a Reformation. Yet, although their Memories will *rot,* there may be some Benefit for their Survivers, to smell it while it is *rotting.*
(*Prose,* 12: 24-25)

Thus, to turn from the poems on Wood's Halfpence or the Delany poems—all of which assume the possibility of reformation—to such poems as "On the Irish-Club" (1730), "The Place of the Damn'd" (1731), "The Day of Judgement" (1731?), "On the Irish Bishops" (1732), "Judas" (1731-32), "The Beasts Confession" (1732), and "The Legion Club" (1736) is to read a poetry of damnation which, if it does anything, records Swift's testimony to the triumph of evil. At the same time, though, these may be hard poems to read, not because they are difficult to understand, but because they virtually reduce the practice of literary criticism to silence. What is there to say, for example, after reading a poem like "The Place of the Damn'd," other than that it is hell to read, and probably was hell to write? The man who in "The Author Upon Himself" (1714) claimed "He reconcil'd Divinity and Wit" (l. 12) is sixteen years later driven to ask himself in "A Dialogue between an eminent Lawyer and Dr. Swift":

> MUST I commend against my conscience
> Such stupid blasphemy and nonsense?
> To such a subject tune my lyre
> And sing like one of MILTON's Choir,
> Where DEVILS to a vale retreat
> And call the laws of wisdom fate,
> Lament upon their hapless fall
> That force free virtue shou'd enthrall?
> (ll. 37-44)

Wherever Swift looks in these later poems he sees devils who represent the culmination of evil, but he can do nothing about them except perform a preliminary damnation in anticipation of their ultimate day of judgment.

As Swift says in "The Place of the Damn'd," "I'll tell you my Mind" (l. 4). Evidently, what is on his mind has very little to do with literary irony and satire, as we can readily see in "The Day of Judgement,"

> I to such Blockheads set my Wit!
> I damn such Fools—Go, go, you're bit!
> (ll. 21-22)

in "On the Irish Bishops,"

> But Courage, my Lords, tho' it cannot be said
> That one *cloven Tongue*, ever set on your Head;
> I'll hold you a Groat, and I wish I cou'd see't,
> If your Stockings were off, you cou'd show *cloven feet*.
> (ll. 49-52)

in "Judas,"

> As antient *Judas by Transgression fell*,
> And *burst asunder* e'er he went to Hell;
> So, could we see a Set of new *Iscariots*,
> Come headlong tumbling from their mitred Chariots,
> (ll. 17-20)

and in the last lines of "The Legion Club," which aptly conclude Swift's poetry of damnation:

> I concluded, looking round 'em,
> May their God, the Devil confound 'em.
> (ll. 241-42)

Perhaps we feel uncomfortable with a writer who drops the literary guise of irony and satire and presumes to damn the world in Old Testament language. Also, in talking about Swift's poetry of damnation we run the risk of raising the specter of Swift's alleged misanthropy. This is certainly the implied conclusion of Leavis's argument when, after commenting that Swift's genius turns life "against itself," he observes: "Here, well on this side of pathology, literary criticism stops" (p. 27). But in his later poems Swift did not turn life against itself; he turned evil against itself by expressing the courage of his convictions. Moreover, this is not a point where literary criticism ought to stop, but where any estimate of Swift's career might well begin.

NOTES

1. "Thoughts on Various Subjects," in *The Prose Works of Jonathan Swift,* ed. Herbert Davis, 14 vols. (Oxford: Blackwell, 1968), 1: 241. Hereafter cited in text as *Prose.*

2. F. R. Leavis, "The Irony of Swift," in *Swift: A Collection of Critical Essays,* ed. Ernest Tuveson (Englewood Cliffs, N.J.: Prentice-Hall, 1964), pp. 15-29. All further page references to this essay are included within the text.

3. *The Correspondence of Alexander Pope,* ed. George Sherburn, 5 vols. (Oxford: Clarendon Press, 1956), 3: 366.

4. See Edward W. Rosenheim, Jr., *Swift and the Satirist's Art* (Chicago: University of Chicago Press, 1963), pp. 12-18, 109-12.

5. For instance, the reason and moderation that Swift recommends in such nonsatirical works as *The Contests and Dissensions in Athens and Rome* and *The Sentiments of a Church-of-England Man* do not, in my view, emerge as forceful "positives" in *A Tale of a Tub* or *Gulliver's Travels.* This is not surprising in *Gulliver's Travels* because Swift knew that he was attacking the definition of man as *animal rationale.* See *The Correspondence of Jonathan Swift,* ed. Sir Harold Williams, 5 vols. (Oxford: Clarendon Press, 1965), 3: 103, 118. Hereafter cited in text as *Corr.*

6. *A Tale of a Tub to which is added The Battle of the Books and The Mechanical Operation of the Spirit,* ed. A. C. Guthkelch and D. Nichol Smith (Oxford: Clarendon Press, 1958), pp. 171-74.

7. On the other hand, Rosenheim has argued that the two famous paragraphs on madness are among the few sources "of whatever fundamental beliefs with respect to morality and metaphysics we can attribute to Swift" (p. 198).

8. "Swift's Poetry Reconsidered," in *English Writers of the Eighteenth Century,* ed. John H. Middendorf (New York: Columbia University Press, 1971), p. 248.

9. "Swift's 'whole Character': The Delany Poems and 'Verses on the Death of Dr. Swift,' " *Modern Language Quarterly* 34 (1973): 415-16.

10. All quotations of Swift's poetry are from *The Poems of Jonathan Swift,* ed. Sir Harold Williams, 3 vols., 2d ed. (Oxford: Clarendon Press, 1958).

15

"A vile Encomium":
That "Panegyric on the Reverend D--n S---t"

AUBREY L. WILLIAMS
University of Florida

Shortly after the turn of this century, in his edition of Swift's correspondence, F. Elrington Ball identified as Swift's[1] a poem in which the Dean is supposed to have adopted the "style & manner" of some "scrub" libels written against him in the years around 1729/30. In this poem, entitled "A Panegyric on the Reverend D--n S---t, In Answer to the Libel on Dr. *D--y*, and a certain Great L—d," Swift is presented as one who privately believes

> That Men of *Wit* can be no more
> Than *Pimps* to Wickedness in *Pow'r*,[2]
> (ll. 25-26)

and also as one who would "think it *little* / To *lick a Rascal Statesman's Spittle*" (ll. 58-59), for had he not, in his "great Devotion" to political sycophancy,

178

Oft' swallow'd down a stronger Potion,
A Composition more absurd,
Bob's [Harley's] *Spittle* mix'd with *Harry's*
    [Bolingbroke's] T---.

                              (ll. 61-63)

Later, Sir Harold Williams, when his edition of Swift's poems appeared in 1937, stated that there "can be little doubt" that Ball was "correct" in seeing the poem as being from Swift's hand (2: 492). Given such assurances, by such authorities, one can only speculate on the attempts that students must make to understand so self-defaming a poem while using as their text, say, the Oxford Standard Authors edition of Swift's *Poetical Works,* in which no question as to the authorship of "A Panegyric on the Reverend D--n S---t" is to be found.

Whatever has been going on in the classroom, there have been, aside from passing allusions to the poem, two fairly recent public attempts to fit "A Panegyric on the Reverend D--n S---t" into propositions about Swift's strategies of poetical self-portraiture. In the first of these, by Robert W. Uphaus, the poem is considered as fitting into "a group of poems in 1730 which begin by attacking Delany's desire for preferment, but which become examinations and affirmations of Swift as a person and a satirist." As a group, these poems ("An Epistle upon an Epistle," "A Libel on Dr. Delany," "A Panegyric on the Reverend D--n S---t," and "Verses on the Death of Dr. Swift") are said to be "extremely important for their uniquely affirmative quality," because they "abruptly depart from the uses of irony we have come to expect from Swift"; to the extent, moreover, "that irony performs a subservient role in these poems, Swift relies far more heavily on a straightforward and aggressive use of autobiography which yields an intensely personal vision: the man, Jonathan Swift, is the poems' matter, and his mind, rather than poetic convention, is the poems' governing form." One problem

with all this immediately appears, however, for having placed
"A Panegyric on the Reverend D--n S---t" in a group of
poems that are said to "abruptly depart from the uses of
irony," Uphaus then goes on to declare that it "is the one
poem in the sequence of Delany poems that does systematically employ irony." Nevertheless, the poem can show us
"just how confident and how sincere Swift is about his own
self-affirmation," for since the narrator of the poem is supposed to be Delany, "to the extent that Delany is taken to
speak these lines with conviction, the irony is reflexive": it
"turns back on Delany" and "we take Swift to be precisely
the reverse of what Delany says." If we understand, finally,
the relation of "A Panegyric on the Reverend D--n S---t" to
the other Delany poems, we will understand the better the
shift in it "from transparent irony to autobiographical assertion."[3]

The second recent assessment of "A Panegyric on the
Reverend D--n S---t" is that made by Louise K. Barnett, who
argues that "clearly, one form that Swift's own self-love takes
is making poetry about himself, although not necessarily
flattering poetry," and who goes on to illustrate her point by
saying, in words that echo, in part at least, Uphaus's view that
"to play his own critic with the vigor demonstrated in 'A
Panegyric on the Reverend Dean *Swift*' is to assert his
strength and self-confidence by outdoing and thus disarming
his real critics. Writing a libel on himself is a way of controlling his enemies' opinions and simultaneously punishing himself for even a fantasied commerce with the devil." The "self"
in Swift's poetry, she believes, "tends to be its own end rather
than a strategy for presenting something else," and so in his
poems "the self is both exalted and ridiculed within a full
spectrum of character possibilities which include the satirist-
hero at one end and the unscrupulous opportunist [as in "A
Panegyric on the Reverend D--n S---t"] at the other."[4]

Such arguments are all very well, and clearly illustrative of the vigor with which critics currently pursue the "presence" of Swift in his work. But suppose, as I believe is the fact, that "A Panegyric on the Reverend D--n S---t" is *not* by Swift. The implications of such a supposition may not be earth-shaking, but certainly they may be cautionary, either for those who find the concept of the persona to be a highly useful instrument in approaches to Swift's poetry, or for those who, following Irvin Ehrenpreis, would find that poetry more directly expressive of various Swiftian "selves." In any event, it seems to me that we should at least review the evidence once more before ascribing to Swift so vile an encomium as "A Panegyric on the Reverend D--n S---t."

In the first place, it should be stressed that attribution of the poem to Swift has been solely a matter of conjecture, an inference from utterly inconclusive data. Never included in his works before this century, it was given to him by Ball and Williams simply because, in their *opinion,* it seems to accord with these words by Swift, in a letter to Lord Bathurst:

> For, having some months ago much & often offended the ruling party, and often worried by libellers I am at the pains of writing one in their style & manner, & sent it by an unknown hand to a Whig printer who very faithfully published it. I took special care to accuse myself but of one fault of which I am really guilty, and so shall continue as I have done these 16 years till I see cause to reform:—but with the rest of the Satyr I chose to abuse myself with the direct reverse of my character or at least in direct opposition to one part of what you are pleased to give me.

A few weeks later Swift informed Gay that a "Scrubb libel," in "the style & Genius of such scoundrels," had been written by himself.[5] It was on the basis of such "hints," as Williams termed the comments in these letters, that "A Panegyric on the Reverend D--n S---t" has been ascribed to Swift.[6]

Understandably so—perhaps. But such an ascription is in

direct conflict, as Williams concedes, with the testimony of
George Faulkner, the printer chosen by Swift himself to
publish his works and who specifically attributed the poem to
James Arbuckle when, in 1768, he prefaced volume 17 of
Swift's *Works* with Arbuckle's "Momus Mistaken, A Fable.
Occasioned by the new Edition of Swift's Works, in 1734,"
and provided this footnote to it:

> This Poem is allowed to be a close Imitation of Dr.
> Swift's manner of writing; the author was acquainted with
> the Dean for many years, and was called by him *Wit Upon
> Crutches,* [7] alluding to his having used them since a boy; he
> was author of Hibernicus's Letters, in 2 vols. and several
> Poetical Pieces, the most admired of which are a
> Panegyrick on Dr. Swift, in answer to a Libel on Dr.
> Delany, and a certain great Lord.

There is, moreover, a copy of "A Panegyric on the Reverend
D--n S---t" bound "in a collection of Arbuckle's published
poems with additional ms. poems," suggesting, in D. F.
Foxon's words, that Faulkner's "attribution to him was correct."[8] In light of such testimony, what are we then to make
of Williams's judgment that "Faulkner was almost certainly
mistaken," not only because of the "hints" provided us in
Swift's letters, but also because "the style" of "A Panegyric
on the Reverend D--n S---t" is "not reminiscent of Arbuckle's known work; Arbuckle, even as a disguise, would
not be likely to include himself among the 'long *unbishoprick'd*' (l. 147), nor speak of himself familiarly in conjunction
with Grattan and Sheridan (l. 177)" (2: 492).

Williams's judgment about such internal components of "A
Panegyric on the Reverend D--n S---t" seems to me to be
either erroneous or beside the mark. In the first place, and
while I would not want to become, or to be considered, an
expert on Arbuckle's work or style, it seems to me that
Williams is wrong when he says the poem "is not reminiscent

of Arbuckle's known work," a judgment I would challenge by way of "Momus Mistaken," a poem acknowledged as Arbuckle's, and about which, we should recall, Faulkner said: "This Poem is allowed to be a close Imitation of Dr. Swift's manner of writing." If Arbuckle could write, in "Momus Mistaken," a "close Imitation" of Swift, we at least should consider, in light of Faulkner's testimony as to the authorship of "A Panegyric on the Reverend D--n S---t," that he could also in that piece have written a close enough "Imitation" of Swift to mislead not only Ball and Williams but also those critics who have followed them.

It appears to me, at any rate, that one can find in "Momus Mistaken" the same kind of snide and bumptious malice that one finds in "A Panegyric on the Reverend D--n S---t," and that though the poem ends with an ostensible compliment to Swift on the publication of his works, it is not until after Swift has been presented, through most of the poem, in a most unsavory light, and additionally accused, in however factitious or shamming terms, of the grossest sexual misconduct. Consider the opening lines of the poem:

> One Day, as is his Wont, the Dean
> Was saunt'ring thro' a dirty Lane;
> And snugly laughing in his Sleeve
> At what would graver Mortals grieve,
> The Crowds of Fools, both low, and high,
> Passing in idle Hurry by.
> *Merc'ry*, 'tis said, to aid his Laughter,
> Follow'd some little Distance after;
> Not in the Shape he wears above,
> Or brings down Messages from *Jove*;
> But in a Form true Politicks
> Will own much fitter for those Tricks,
> Of Theft, the God did whilom use;
> A Black-guard Crier of the News.
>   What Conversation pass'd between
> This merry Pair in such a Scene;
> What waggish Jokes, and sly Remarks

On City Damsels, and their Sparks,
The Muse at present hath forgot;
Nor is't esential to her Plot.
But sure 'twould form, of Mirth, a Tale,
Might *Pope,* and all his Friends regale.
Nor he, nor they would blush to sit,
And shake at such odd Strains of Wit.[9]

(ll. 1-24)

The "compliments" to Swift (if they are to be considered such) are actually of a most vile and disingenuous sort, and of the same heavily insinuative mode of "A Panegyric on the Reverend D--n S---t": Swift, in a "dirty Lane" (l. 2), snickers at what would make "graver Mortals grieve" (l. 4); relishes the scandalmongery of a "Black-guard Crier" (l. 14) of the town; savors, along with Pope and other friends, salacious tidbits about "City Damsels, and their Sparks" (l. 18) that would presumably put other folks to a "blush" (l. 23) they themselves are too hardened to raise. And when Momus, the god of blame and ridicule, then enters and supposedly mistakes Swift for "*Apollo* in Disguise" (l. 42), the Dean is handled in an even more scurrilous manner. Why, asks Momus, would he be "in such a scurvy Place" (l. 49), equipped with Mercury, his "Scoundrel Pimp" (l. 51), unless he had "some *Daphne* in the Wind" (l. 48)? And Momus goes on:

Can no Misfortunes in Amours
Suffice to put an End to yours?
Perhaps you think, you're Woman Proof,
And always will come safely off;
Or hope to be no more affronted,
Than when you after *Daphne* hunted;
Where *Fortune,* to prevent a Quarrel,
Your Misadventure crown'd with Laurel.

(ll. 55-62)

The precise import of Momus's jibes at Swift is probably indeterminable, though one may wonder if he aims at the Dean's familiarity with some particular "Daphne." Both Mrs. Pilkington and Lady Acheson have been thought the subject of his two poems, "Death and Daphne" and "Daphne" (3: 902–3). In any event, the greater part of the poem consists of nasty associations of Swift with low and lecherous motives, while the lip service paid to the publication of his works in the last few lines, especially since it comes from the mouth of his "Scoundrel Pimp" and a "Black-guard Crier of the News," scarcely makes amends for the scurvy treatment accorded the Dean in the body of the poem. "Momus Mistaken," in my opinion, is a poem very much in the style and manner of "A Panegyric on the Reverend D--n S---t."

As to Williams's other points, it seems to me sufficient to point out that the allusions to "A Libel on Dr. Delany," in "A Panegyric on the Reverend D--n S---t," scarcely of themselves "suggest parody by Swift rather than by another hand," for as Williams himself observes elsewhere, Delany's maladroit appeal for further patronage, and Swift's friendly ridicule of that appeal, had made the whole affair the talk of the town and had inspired other writers "to bait the unfortunate Delany."[10] His comment that Arbuckle, "even as a disguise would not be likely to include himself among the 'long *unbishoprick'd*' (l. 147), nor speak of himself familiarly in conjunction with Grattan and Sheridan (l. 177)," is equally beside the mark, for the supposed speaker of "A Panegyric on the Reverend D--n S---t" is Delany, a cleric and a friend of Grattan and Sheridan, not Arbuckle *in propia persona*. Donning the mask of a toadylike Delany, it is quite within the fictive context of the poem for Arbuckle to present Delany as ludicrously lamenting his lack of preferment.

When we turn to "A Panegyric on the Reverend D--n S---t" itself, we must, if we are to consider Swift to be its author on the grounds offered by Ball and Williams, first suppose that he entered into the mind and character, the "style & Genius," of a scoundrelly scrub libeler, and then, from that vantage point (if so it may be called), proceeded to fashion the character of a sycophantic Patrick Delany whose "voice" in its turn is made to "abuse" Swift, the "real" author of the poem, "with the direct reverse" of his actual character. This is pretty complicated, it seems to me, either for those who would see Swift as in some way distanced from his work by means of masks or personae, or for those who see a more or less direct revelation of "self" in that work. For myself, I simply cannot believe that Swift, however stinging the preceptive raillery he directed at Delany elsewhere, would have constructed for his friend a persona that is so toadying and self-serving as that of the supposed "narrator" of this poem—one who solicits Swift to teach such "little Folks" (l. 1) as himself the "Science" (l. 28) of pimping "to Wickedness in *Power*" (1. 26). The direction of the satire, we should note, always points two ways: not only toward Swift, the master "Pimp," but also toward a fawning circle of friends who would eagerly abandon "musty Rules" (l. 29) and "idle Morals" (l. 30) in emulation of their corrupt, and corruptive, mentor. I can, on the other hand, believe the portrait of Delany to have been fashioned by one who was a primary object of Swift's aversion,[11] by one who may have thought himself severely handled by Swift in a poem published only a few weeks before the appearance of "A Panegyric on the Reverend D--n S---t,"[12] by one who was "a hack of the Government who employed his feeble pen to meet Swift's attack" on that government,[13] by one who in 1725 had celebrated from Dublin the birthday of George I in such fulsome terms as these:

> No Poet's Breast did e'er with Raptures glow
> More warm, than We to our Great Monarch owe;

No Monarch e'er beheld a People more
Dispos'd to hail, and bless his natal Hour.[14]

The portrait of Swift that emerges from "A Panegyric on
the Reverend D--n S---t," is indeed an "ignoble" one, as
Barnett says. But it has been drawn, I believe, not by Swift
himself, but by one whose animus is unrelievedly poisonous
and spiteful, and by one who has tried to make Swift's own
words and works revile him. It also seems to me unlikely in
the highest degree that Swift would present himself, even
ironically, as one who oft had "swallow'd down" (l. 61)

Bob's Spittle mix'd with *Harry's* T.
(l. 63)

Leaving aside the utterly nasty denigration of Swift himself
(one devoid of any irony, as far as I can tell) in such lines,
there is also the utterly nasty denigration of his association
with two long-time friends, the deceased Robert Harley, and
Bolingbroke, with whom Swift was still on terms of polite if
distant amity. Neither here nor elsewhere in the poem do we
seem to be given the slightest hint that all this, Uphaus's
reading to the contrary, is to be taken as "transparent irony,"
that the poem *is* a parody, that the characterizations of Swift
and his friends are to be taken in some inversive way. Would
Swift have so denigrated himself, and so impugned his
friends, just to prove he *could* write a parody of some "scrub
libeller," or just for fun? And what would be the point of it
all, in any case, of doing so anonymously, with no point of
disclosure that all the scurrilous contumely is to be taken as
irony or parody? This last seems to me a crucial point, for
even Ehrenpreis, whatever his depreciation of critical stress
on the persona concept, yet seems to admit of what he calls
the "ironical persona," though only such a one "that is
intended to be seen through, a mask that the reader at first

supposes to be genuine but at last sees removed." It "must grow obvious," he says, "that the author himself is not in earnest, but is delivering a parody, acting out a caricature of a type of man he loathes or contemns"—"an ironical hoaxer must show himself if his device is to succeed."[15] I do not share Ehrenpreis's objections to recent critical emphasis on the persona concept, but if we are to suppose that "A Panegyric on the Reverend D--n S---t" is from Swift's own hand, then I think we would also have to say that the poem fails to meet even Ehrenpreis's criteria for a successful parody or hoax. If Swift himself, again supposing him the author, was relying on some kind of antiphrastic irony to come through his words, then he has, for me at least, failed dismally and uncharacteristically.

There are many poems in which Swift presents himself, or is presented by other speakers, as awkward, officious, abrasive, vain, censorious, and so on, but in none of these is he presented, by whatever mode or spokesman, as guilty of the downright impiety and godlessness, the appalling sycophancy, the secret villainy, the totally unscrupulous self-seeking and time-serving, heaped upon him in "A Panegyric on the Reverend D--n S---t." One may contend, of course, that this only suggests how masterfully he has painted the kind of portrait of himself that the kind of "Delany" painted by a kind of "scrub libeller" would have wanted to paint. One may find, with Uphaus, that the poem, when read in relation to the other Delany poems, is indeed a "transparent irony" throughout, or agree with Barnett that Swift in this poem chose to confess the "flawed reality" of himself. For my part, I cannot help but think that Faulkner was right in his attribution of the poem to a man whom Swift despised, but who was "allowed" by his contemporaries as capable of producing "a close Imitation of Dr. Swift's manner of writing." I also, in the end, cannot help but think that Swift had too much self-esteem, and too much kindness toward his friends, to write a poem from which he would exclude any hint of irony in so vile and defamatory a portrayal of himself, and of them, as is to be found in "A Panegyric on the Reverend D--n S---t."[16]

NOTES

1. *The Correspondence of Jonathan Swift, D. D.,* 6 vols. (London: G. Bell and Sons, 1910-14), 4: 167n.

2. All quotations of Swift's poetry are taken from *The Poems of Jonathan Swift,* ed. Sir Harold Williams, 3 vols., 2d ed. (Oxford: Clarendon Press, 1958).

3. "Swift's 'Whole Character': The Delany Poems and 'Verses on the Death of Dr. Swift,' " *Modern Language Quarterly* 34 (1973): 406, 409, 410.

4. "Fictive Self-Portraiture in Swift's Poetry," a paper presented to a Special Session on Swift's poetry at the annual MLA meeting, Chicago, 1977.

5. See *The Correspondence of Jonathan Swift,* ed. Sir Harold Williams, 5 vols. (Oxford: Clarendon Press, 1963-65), 3: 410-11; 418.

6. But as Phillip Harth noted, in his "Response" to an MLA Special Session in New York, December 1978, on "The Contexts of Swift's Poetry" (at which the original version of the present paper was presented), the length to which Sir Harold Williams was forced to go in such an ascribing of "A Panegyric on the Reverend D--n S---t" to Swift himself is indicated by the fact that he first argued (see *Poems,* 2: 493n.) that the "one fault" at which Swift supposedly "hints" in his letter is to be found in lines 17-20 of the poem, "where 'Delany' accuses him of managing to profit from every 'Wind of Favour.' " Harth goes on: "This was so unlucky a guess that Sir Harold Williams was eventually forced to abandon it. In 1963, when he published the first three volumes of Swift's *Correspondence,* he made another stab at it which was even less fortunate. This time he chose lines 77-79 of the poem where, as he explained, 'Swift declares himself deficient in wit' [3: 411n.]. Now if there is one fault to which Swift would never have confessed, it is surely that of being deficient in wit!"

7. "Wit upon Crutches," a broadside poetic invective against Arbuckle in which his infirmity is not spared, was reprinted in *Gulliveriana* (London, 1728), and was attributed to Swift by Ball, with whom Williams disagrees (See *Poems,* 3: 1127-28). But as Harth notes in his MLA "Response," Swift's enemy, Jonathan Smedley, had attributed (in the table of contents of *Gulliveriana*) "Wit upon Crutches" to "Gulliver," a clear signal, to Arbuckle perhaps, that the poem was indeed by Swift.

8. See *English Verse, 1701-1750,* 2 vols., (Cambridge: Cambridge University Press, 1975), 1: 552 (items P36, P37). Foxon's entry was called to my attention by James Woolley.

9. I quote from the broadside (Dublin: Printed in the Year 1735). See Foxon, 1: A282.

10. *Poems,* 2: 486-87.

11. See F. Elrington Ball, *Swift's Verse: An Essay* (London: John Murray, 1929), pp. 180-81, 203.

12. In his MLA "Response," Harth suggests that Arbuckle would have had reason to believe that Swift had attacked him not only in "Wit upon Crutches" (1725), but also in "A Funeral Apotheosis on the Tribunes," published in Dublin only a few weeks before "A Panegyric on the Reverend D--n S---t" (see *Poems,* 3: 1133). As Harth says, "A note in this later lampoon on Arbuckle declares: 'The Publick need not have any Hint as to the Author; the peculiar Marks of his Genius appearing very evidently in it.' In other words, while pretending to refrain from any hint, the publisher gives the broadest possible hint that Swift is the author of this satire. If Arbuckle was misled into believing that his old enemy had attacked him once again, he would have had every reason to reply at once with such a poem as 'A Panegyrick on the Reverend D--n S---t.' "

13. See Henry Craik, *The Life of Jonathan Swift,* 2d ed., 2 vols. (New York: Burt Franklin, 1969; 1st published 1894), 2: 184.

14. "A New Prologue, On the Anniversary of his Majesty K. *George.*" I quote from the broadside (Dublin: Printed by J. Carson in Coghill's Court, Dames-street, 1725). See Foxon, 1: A285.

15. "Personae," in *Restoration and Eighteenth-Century Literature,* ed. Carroll Camden (Chicago: University of Chicago Press, 1963), pp. 34, 35, 36.

16. I wish to express my appreciation to Ms. Gisela Casines, my graduate research assistant, for the many ways in which she has helped me in the preparation of this essay.

primarily the National Library of Wales volume to which
Foxon and Williams refer, persuasively supports the judgment
that Swift did not write "A Panegyric." Its deceptively
Swiftian style comes simply from its being a parody of
Swift's "Libel on D[r.] D[elany]."

In surveying the evidence, I shall show, first, that the
National Library of Wales volume constitutes in effect the
testimony of a knowledgeable eighteenth-century reader that
the "Panegyric" is Arbuckle's; second, that an analysis of
handwriting and textual variants reveals that reader to be
Arbuckle himself; and third, that George Faulkner's independent testimony as to Arbuckle's authorship is likely to be
correct. Finally, I shall point to what is probably the true
scrub libel.

Some scholars, perhaps unduly influenced by "Momus
Mistaken," not one of Arbuckle's happiest poetic efforts,
have doubted that he was even capable of writing the
"Panegyric," and he has been inaccurately labeled a government hack.[3] On the contrary, he was an intelligent, literate
essayist not without significance in the history of eighteenth-
century philosophy: he has been viewed as a link between
Shaftesbury and the Scottish philosophers, particularly Francis Hutcheson.[4] He was a competent versifier, producing
burlesque poems as well as translations and imitations.[5]

About 1724, arriving in Dublin from his studies at the
University of Glasgow, Arbuckle came under the influence of
Robert, first Viscount Molesworth, a Shaftesburian and
Swift's ally in the Wood's halfpence controversy. Molesworth
gathered under his tutelage a small group that included Arbuckle and Hutcheson, then a Dublin schoolmaster. At
Molesworth's house these young men wrote many of the
essays Arbuckle published in his series, Hibernicus's Letters,
which appeared in the *Dublin Weekly Journal* (1725-27). As
Hibernicus, Arbuckle made a major contribution to Dublin
literary and intellectual life, sufficiently effective to earn

several gibes in the broadside verse of the day. In 1729 he attempted a single-essay periodical, the *Tribune*. (Though nearly all present authorities give authorship of this periodical to Patrick Delany, following a mistaken attribution in 1777, contemporary testimony is unanimous that the author was Arbuckle.)[6] Some of his poems are collected in *The Edinburgh Miscellany* (1720); others, published separately, are listed by Foxon.

To these must be added, I shall argue, all the manuscript poems in the previously mentioned volume held in the Department of Printed Books, National Library of Wales (PR 4116 A47 [DE 6057-60]). This volume, bound in eighteenth-century paneled calf, contains four printed poems and another thirty-three in manuscript. It would appear to have been unknown to all writers on Swift or Arbuckle before Foxon, having been discarded as a duplicate (!) by the British Museum Department of Printed Books in 1914. The volume contains no mark of prior ownership and, with four exceptions to be noted, no indication of the authorship of the poems. The binder's label simply says "POEMS."[7]

Three of the printed poems are identified as Arbuckle's on their title pages; the fourth is a London edition of *A Panegyric*. Of the thirty-three manuscript poems, fourteen can be independently attributed to Arbuckle, usually from attributions in *The Edinburgh Miscellany* (EM) or in Hibernicus's Letters (HL). These seventeen are marked with an asterisk (*) in the following list.

CONTENTS OF THE NATIONAL LIBRARY OF WALES VOLUME

Snuff, a Poem, by Mr. James Arbuckle. Edinburgh: printed by M'Euen for the Author, 1719. [Several manuscript corrections.]

An Epistle to the . . . Earl of Hadington, on the Death of Joseph Addison, Esq. By James Arbuckle, A.M. in the

University of Glasgow. London: printed for M'Euen in Edinburgh and Cox in London, 1719. [A few manuscript corrections.]

Glotta, a Poem. Humbly Inscribed to . . . the Marquess of Carnarvon. By Mr. Arbuckle, Student in the University of Glasgow. Glasgow: Duncan, 1721. [A few manuscript corrections.]

A Panegyric on the Reverend Dean Swift. In Answer to a Libel on Dr. Delany, and a Certain Great Lord. Never Before Printed. London: printed for J. Roberts & N. Blandford, 1730. [Extensive manuscript corrections.]

Uniform in the same binding, seventy-five pages of manuscript follow immediately, all in the same hand except for the last twelve pages (beginning with "To Celia"):

*An Epistle to Mr Thomas Griffith of Rhual in the County of Flint. Glasgow College May 12th 1720. [Concludes with rhyming signature "James Arbuckle."]

*Psalm CIV. Paraphrased in Imitation of Milton's Stile. [Printed as Arbuckle's in HL 18 (31 July 1725); for the authorship of the individual contributions to HL, see No. 102 (25 March 1727).]

Psalm CIII.

Psalm CXXXIX.

Psalm VIII.

*Horace, Book III. Ode 3. [Quoted in Arbuckle's HL 78 (24 September 1726).]

*Horace, Epod II. [Printed as Arbuckle's in HL 88 (3 December 1726).]

Horace, Book II. Ode 10. Imitated.

From the French of Mr. Des Barreaux.

*Horace, Book II. Ode 18 [Printed in Arbuckle's HL 59 (14 May 1726). Like the "Panegyric," this translation has been erroneously attributed to Swift. See Swift, *Works*, ed. Sir Walter Scott, 2d ed. (Edinburgh: Constable, 1824), 1: 31; and F. Elrington Ball, *Swift's Verse: An Essay* (London: Murray, 1929), pp. 32, 38.]

*Horace, Book I. Ode 28. [Printed as Arbuckle's in HL 59 (14 May 1726).]

Horace, Book III. Ode 9.

*The same imitated. [Printed as Arbuckle's in EM, pp. 57–59.]

*Prologue to Tamerlaine at the acting of it by several young Gentlemen of the University of Glasgow in Dec.ʳ 1720. [Printed as Arbuckle's in *Prologue and Epilogue to Tamerlaine. Acted in the Grammar School in Glasgow, December 30th, 1720: By the Students of the University* (Glasgow: Duncan, 1721). See also *A Short Account of the Late Treatment of the Students of the University of Glasgow* (Dublin, 1722), pp. 18–19. Copies of both are in the University of Glasgow Library.]

To Mʳ John Smith. [Smith was one of Arbuckle's cohorts in a struggle against the University of Glasgow authorities; see *A Short Account,* pp. 27–39.]

*Horace, Book I. Ode 13. [Printed as Arbuckle's in EM, pp. 204–5, and in HL 66 (2 July 1726).]

*Horace, Book III. Ode 29. [Printed as Arbuckle's in EM, pp. 209–13, and in HL 66 (2 July 1726).]

Horace, Book I. Ode 32.

A Translation of part of the Ninth Book of Lucan's Pharsalia.

Written in Milton's Paradise Regain'd.

Fragment from Cornelius Gallus.

To My Lord Molesworth, on perusal of his Daughter, Mrs. [Mary] Mon[c]k's, poems. [Molesworth, Arbuckle's patron, had published her poems in 1717.]

*Horace, Book III. Ode 6. [Published as Arbuckle's in EM, pp. 155–58.]

On Captain Forrester's travelling in the Highlands of Scotland in Winter. [Anonymously printed in a Dublin broadside, undated, Foxon P564; and in Faulkner's *London and Dublin Magazine* for July 1734, dating the travel 1731; see also John Hill Burton, *Life and Correspondence of David Hume* (Edinburgh, 1846), 1: 174–75.]

On Sir Isaac Newton. [Transcript dated "Exeter Sept. 8 1731" in Bodleian MS Rawl. poet. 207, p. 171.]

*Momus Mistaken. A Fable occasioned by [the] New Edition of Dean Swif[t's] Works. 1734. [Signed broadside published by Faulkner, 1735.]

Prologue Spoken at the Theatre Royal in Dublin 30th October 1734. Being his Majesty's Birth-Day.

To Celia presenting the Author a looking Glass.

Verses occasioned by a late Play-Bill wherein a new Ass is promised to come upon the Stage.

A Proper New Ballad on the celebrated Miss Molly Rowe, To the Tune of Molly Mog.

*To Mr. Allen [sic] Ramsay on the Publication of his Works. [Published as Arbuckle's in Ramsay's *Poems* (Edinburgh, 1720).]

*Prologue to Cato, Spoke in Glasgow May 28th 1719. [Published as Arbuckle's in EM, pp. 79–81.]

On Swift's Leaving his Fortune to Build a Mad-House. [Swift's bequest was announced in the *Dublin Journal*, 18–21 January 1734/5. This poem was published in *A Collection of Epigrams*, vol. 2 (London, 1737).]

From the foregoing list it is a reasonable inference that this volume was intended—by whomever transcribed and compiled—to be a collection of the poems of James Arbuckle. Although none of the manuscript poems carries a formal statement of authorship, almost half can be identified as his by other evidence; and expressed as a proportion of total pages, the part of the manuscript independently attributable to him is much greater. As for the remaining poems, a search for attributions revealed none to anyone else.[8] In style and genre they are like Arbuckle's known work. Two are addressed to known associates of his. The occasional poems reflect the Glasgow milieu of his Glasgow years and the Dublin milieu of his Dublin years. For all these reasons, this volume probably was intended by its knowledgeable compiler as a collection of James Arbuckle's poems, and the physically integral presence of *A Panegyric* in the volume amounts to informed contemporary testimony that Arbuckle wrote the poem.

In the nature of things it would not be unlikely for an

anonymous single-author collection of manuscript poems to have been formed by the poet himself. Handwriting and textual variants confirm that Arbuckle was the compiler in this case. With the National Library of Wales (NLW) manuscript I have compared a sample of Arbuckle's handwriting from his youth—a letter to Lord Molesworth of 13 October 1722,[9] and two later samples: his letters of 1737 to the Rev. Thomas Drennan, now in the Public Record Office of Northern Ireland (PRONI), and pages apparently in Arbuckle's hand from a Quit Rent Office (QRO) letterbook dating from the period when he was a clerk in that office.[10] Arbuckle's writing is a version of the "round" hand standard in copybooks of the time. However, the Arbuckle samples share numerous peculiarities which distinguish his hand from others formed on the same model. The early sample is closer to the smooth curves and graceful proportions of a copybook; the PRONI and QRO samples are closer to the later writing in the NLW manuscript, though the QRO handwriting is sometimes hastier and less controlled.

A full analytical description of Arbuckle's handwriting would be far beyond the scope of this article, but a few illustrative particulars may at least be suggestive. Among the various samples there are similarities in letter forms, letter spacing, and execution of common letter groups. These similarities show that the interlinear changes in the NLW copy of *A Panegyric* are in the same hand as the NLW manuscript in the same volume (Figs. 1–3, 11, 14). Further, they show that the hand of the NLW manuscript is the same as that in Arbuckle's letters to Molesworth and Drennan and in the QRO letterbook. One peculiarity of Arbuckle's hand is the ligature between the **o** and **f** of **of** (Fig. 4). Another unusual feature is a preliminary ornamental loop in the **L** (Fig. 5); in later samples he uses a more conventional concluding loop, often irregular in its curve (Fig. 6). All the samples show characteristic formations of the words **your,**

FIG. 1

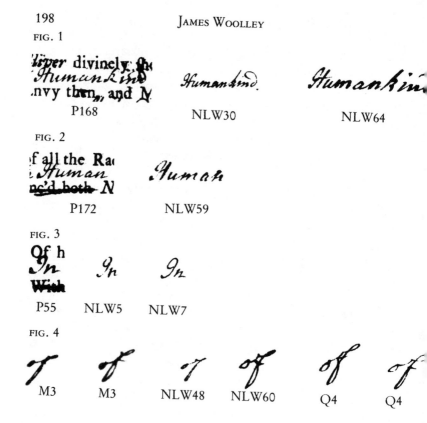

P168

NLW30

NLW64

FIG. 2

P172

NLW59

FIG. 3

P55   NLW5   NLW7

FIG. 4

M3   M3   NLW48   NLW60   Q4   Q4

KEY

Reproductions are approximately actual size.

D   Arbuckle's letters to Drennan + page number

M   Arbuckle's letter to Molesworth + page number

NLW   National Library of Wales Arbuckle manuscript + page number

P   Arbuckle's annotated *Panegyric* + line number

Q   Quit Rent Office letterbook + folio number (or, if followed by *o.e.*, page number counting from the other end of the book)

FIG. 5

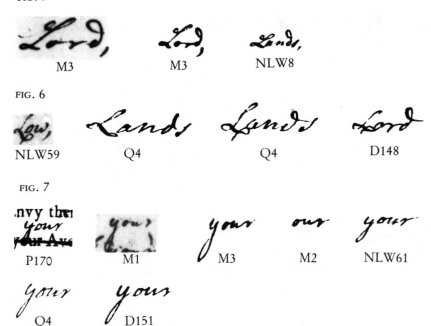

M3   M3   NLW8

FIG. 6

NLW59   Q4   Q4   D148

FIG. 7

P170   M1   M3   M2   NLW61

Q4   D151

In **your** Arbuckle often lifts his pen before the pattern **our**; he stretches slightly between the **u** and the **r**, letting the downward stroke of the **r** fall slightly below the line.

FIG. 8

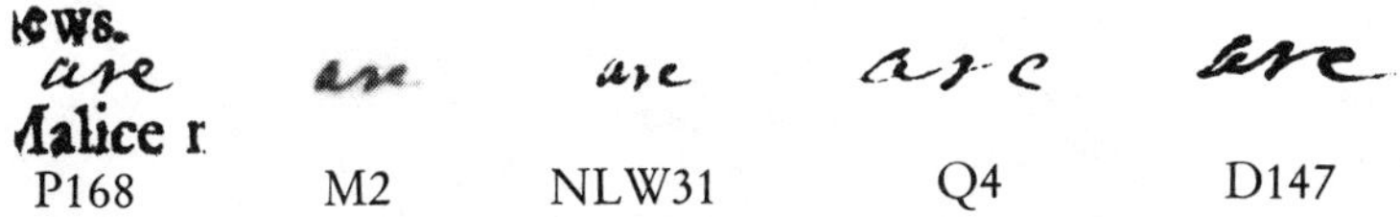

P168   M2   NLW31   Q4   D147

The **a** often begins with a small loop or upward motion, the downstroke of the **r** falling below the line of writing.

FIG. 9

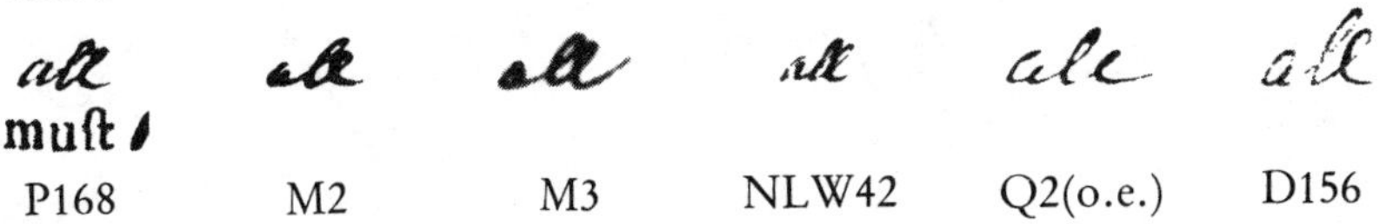

P168   M2   M3   NLW42   Q2(o.e.)   D156

FIG. 10

M3   M3   NLW63   Q4   D147

FIG. 11

lone of
. Coth.
renoun

P172   NLW58   NLW30   D158   NLW58   Q4   D158

FIG. 12

M3   NLW60   Q1(o.e.)

FIG. 13

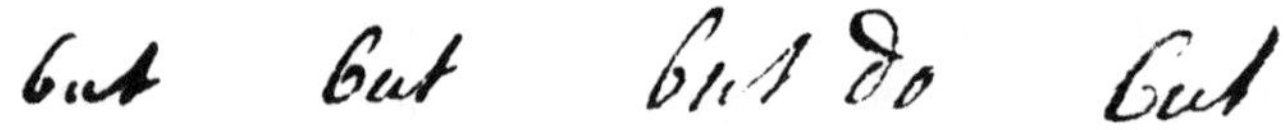

M3   NLW59   Q1(o.e.)   D156

FIG. 14

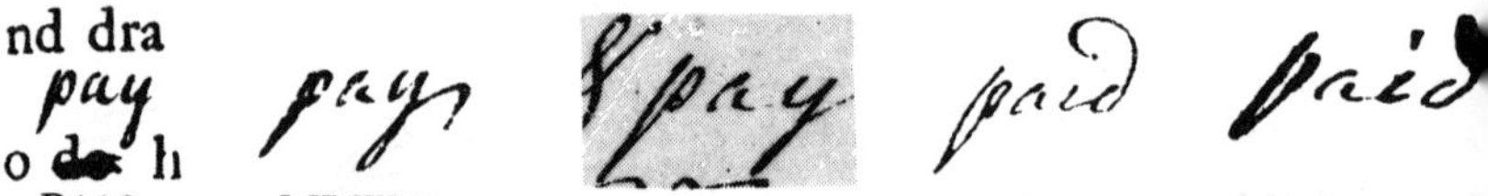

nd dra
pay
o do h

P112   NLW63   Q4   Q4   Q4

D148

FIG. 15

NLW59   NLW62   Q1(o.e.)   Q2(o.e.)

are, and all (Figs. 7–9). Arbuckle's th is characteristic and consistent (Figs. 10–11). His b can be formed like a 6, with the bottom curving up around to the left toward the vertical downstroke; the loop of the ascender is often incomplete, so that for him the b is often an ungainly letter (Figs. 11–13). The delta d is seldom very graceful in its curve, and the tail sometimes crosses itself higher than is usual in writing on this model (Fig. 5–6, 12–14). According to the copybooks, the descender of the p should consist of two close parallel lines joined in a curve at the bottom; Arbuckle instead forms a V, often crooked (Fig. 14). There are striking similarities between the numerals in the NLW manuscript and those in the QRO letterbook (Fig. 15). The chances that all these characteristics would appear in any other person's handwriting are remote.

The longer one studies such parallels, the more firmly one is convinced that the altered copy of *A Panegyric* in the National Library of Wales is Arbuckle's own revision. In effect, this volume stands as his tacit claim to have written the poem, a claim the more persuasive because it is unlikely to have been made to deceive.

Analysis of textual variants in the poem and in the whole volume substantiates Arbuckle's authorship. Most of the manuscript alterations to the *Panegyric* change it to agree with the Dublin edition, but a few substantive readings occur in no printed edition and are apparently authorial.[11] And comparison of the manuscript poems with their printed versions reveals extensive substantive variation in almost every case: this manuscript was not compiled by mere copying from available printed sources. Its substantial revisions are the sort an author would make.

George Faulkner attributes "A Panegyric" to Arbuckle in the preliminaries to volume 17 of his editions of Swift's *Works* (1768). His knowledge would have come from the fact that he himself had had a commercial interest in the Delany poems. It has not, I think, been previously noticed that on the evidence of the printer's ornaments *A Libel on D— D—* and many associated poems can be shown to have come from Faulkner's press.[12] In the small literary world of Dublin in 1730, Faulkner would have had reason to be aware of who wrote what. His authority about Swift's canon also comes from his direct role in planning the 1735 edition of the *Works*. Further, Faulkner had at least some contact with Arbuckle, since he published *Momus Mistaken* in 1735.

Other things being equal, each of the kinds of evidence I have discussed would tend to suggest that Arbuckle wrote "A Panegyric." Together they amount to very strong support for the conclusion reached by Aubrey L. Williams.

But if Arbuckle wrote the "Panegyric," where is the poem Swift said he wrote against himself? From his letters to Bathurst (Oct. 1730) and Gay (10 Nov. 1730) we may draw several clues. The work we seek is a "scrub libel," indeed "a very scrub one in verses lately written by myself." It is in the "style & manner" of the "libellers" who had "often worryed" Swift several months earlier, when he had "much & often offended the ruling party" with "A Libel on D— D—": Swift alludes here to the controversy over his receiving the freedom of Dublin in a gold box.[13] The poem was "sent . . . by an unknown hand to a Whig printer [in Dublin] who very faithfully published it"; it was "reprinted in London." The negative characterization of Swift was somewhat extensive: "I took special care to accuse myself but of one fault of which I am really guilty, and so shall continue as I have done these sixteen years [since Queen Anne's death] till I see cause to reform:—but with the rest of the Satyr I chose to abuse myself with the direct reverse of my character or at least in direct opposition to one part of what you are pleased to give me," Swift tells Lord Bathurst. About the date of composition Swift is ambiguous; he says in October that the poem was "lately written," and at least it seems reasonable to believe that the scrub libel was one of the later poems in the whole group surrounding Delany's quest for preferment in 1729 and 1730.

From Swift's own comments it is manifest that the poem was a burlesque attack on himself and that it was associated with the controversy surrounding Delany. Because the poem burlesqued anti-Swift poems, both in style and in matter, it will be hard to distinguish it from a real anti-Swift poem. Nevertheless, Foxon's *English Verse, 1701-1750* lists six other poems against Swift, each associated with the Delany controversy and published in Dublin in late 1729 or 1730. One of these is likely to be Swift's scrub libel. (It seems improbable that Swift's poem has not survived, since it was printed at least twice, both in Dublin and London, and was about a subject as important as Swift.)

The following five, though plausible candidates, are *not*, I think, the scrub libel:[14]

An Answre to the Christmass-Box. In Defence of Docter D—n—y. By R-t B-r. Dublin, 1729. Only incidentally against Swift; too early (around Christmas 1729); and on the evidence of the typography and ornaments, printed not by a Whig but by Swift's regular printer until this time, Sarah Harding. (This pamphlet seems to be the last Sarah Harding printing.)

A Letter of Advice to the Revd. D--r. D--la--y, Humbly Propos'd to the Consideration of a Certain Great Lord. [Dublin, ?1729.] Only incidentally against Swift, and too early, since it follows directly Delany's *An Epistle to Lord Carteret,* published before 6 December 1729, when it was reprinted in the *Old Dublin Intelligence.* Apparently *A Letter of Advice* was not reprinted in London.

Some Seasonable Advice to Doctor D—n—y. [Dublin], 1730. The attack on Swift is merely for overpraising Delany and does not present a character of him. Apparently not reprinted in London.

Advice to a Certain Dean. [Dublin], 1730. Attacks Swift for

"A Libel on D— D—" but presents no character of him. Apparently not reprinted in London.

An Epistle to D—n S—t. In Answer to a Lible [*sic*] *on D— D— and a Certain Great Lord.* [Dublin], 1730. Though anti-Swift, with allusions to "A Libel" and plagiarism from Smedley's "An Epistle to . . . Grafton" (1724; *Poems*, 2: 357), the poem survives in only one reported copy (see Foxon E396), suggesting a smaller initial printing than one would have expected. The poem was apparently never reprinted in London, and indeed it is so wretchedly, non-sensically, dully bad that its being reprinted is hardly conceivable. This poem is incoherent, whereas Swift's scrub libel was sufficient coherent that he felt he had to warn his friends not to take it seriously. Though this is possibly the poem Swift wrote, there is a much better candidate.

Of six anti-Swift poems, the likeliest to be the scrub libel is the anonymous *An Answer to Dr. D—y's Fable of the Pheasant and the Lark* ([Dublin], 1730). It was first attributed to Swift in 1765 by Deane Swift, perhaps on the basis of the poet's own manuscript or printed copy, and it will be found in all subsequent editions of Swift (see *Poems*, 2: 507-15). It has an extensive unfavorable character of Swift (lines 63-107). It was indeed reprinted in London, in the *Daily Post-Boy* of 17 June 1730 (*Poems*, 2: 507), and that date and other evidence suggest that it was one of the later poems in the Delany controversy.

Commentators have almost ignored the poem.[15] This is probably because it makes little sense unless one sees it as a burlesque: the poem mocks Delany and Swift as though one of their enemies had written it. Taken straightforwardly, the heavy attack on Delany's "Fable" (e.g., ll. 1-32 of the "Answer" mock ll. 1-10 of the "Fable") seems odd coming from a Swift who at about the same time is working to comfort Delany (*Poems*, 2: 499-506); and the attack is at points unscrupulous: Delany does not say that the peacock grew rich and wise by having his eyes in his tail ("Answer," ll. 17-18), but rather that his "eyes" were an "Emblem" of the "Train" of "that Monarch," that is, George II. Nor does Delany say that the peacock was chosen "for Flight and Voice" ("Answer," l. 20). Moreover, Swift concludes the poem with a triplet, though he disapproved of triplets and had used the triplet for burlesque effect in "A Description of a City Shower" (1710).[16] Burlesque also seems to be the point of the triplets in "The Life and Genuine Character of Doctor Swift," particularly if one accepts Laetitia Pilkington's view that Swift meant to "burlesque himself" in that poem (*Poems*, 2: 542-43).

When Swift tells Bathurst that in the scrub libel he accuses himself "but of one fault of which I am really guilty," it is clear from the context that he refers to his opposition to the Whig domination since 1714. In the "Answer" reference to this "fault" appears in such statements as that Swift "against the Court is always blabbing" (l. 70). Otherwise he accuses himself of faults embodying "the direct reverse of [his] character": namely, that his "Wit . . . is gone"; that he writes only out of "Spleen and Spite"; that he "thinks the Nation always err'd,/ Because himself is not preferr'd"; that his reference to Queen Caroline in "A Libel on D— D—" is malicious; that Lord Allen's accusations about "A Libel" are justified; that Swift is a "publick Foe" and an "Enemy of human Kind"; that he "daily vends seditious Trash" (at the time Swift was complaining of an abundance of false attributions to him); that "in the Praise of Virtue [he] is dumb" (though "A Libel" had included a paean to Pope's virtue); that he can write neither prose nor verse; that out of sheer malice he would have Ireland lose her "English Friends"; and that he "never had one publick Thought,/ Nor ever gave the Poor a Groat." This poem may deserve neglect—its ironic point of view is not successfully established—but it fits

Swift's description of his scrub libel. Though by 1730 Swift's Dublin printing was being done by George Faulkner, there is some evidence that Aaron Rhames printed *An Answer*, suggesting that, as Swift said, he did not in this case employ his usual printer.[17]

The available evidence points to "An Answer to Dr. Delany's Fable of the Pheasant and the Lark" as being Swift's "scrub libel" upon himself. More abundant evidence confirms that the "Panegyric on the Reverend Dean Swift," which had seemed to be Swift's flamboyant self-excoriation, should be removed from his canon and given to James Arbuckle. Some time ago a distinguished critic of eighteenth-century literature remarked to me that if Swift did not write "A Panegyric," he might well have written it. Whether this view in fact adequately embodies our understanding of Swift the man and the poet now requires a careful reconsideration.[18]

NOTES

1. Aubrey L. Williams, " 'A vile Encomium': That 'Panegyric on the Reverend D--n S---t,' " read at MLA in December 1978 and printed in the present volume. In "Jonathan Swift: The Presentation of Self in Doggerel Rhyme" (read at the Clark Memorial Library, January 1979), Robert C. Elliott viewed Williams's conclusions skeptically and asked for stronger evidence against Swift's authorship. See also D. F. Foxon, *English Verse, 1701-1750,* 2 vols. (London: Cambridge University Press, 1975), P36. W. B. Carnochan had expressed a doubt about Swift's authorship in *Lemuel Gulliver's Mirror for Man* (Berkeley: University of California Press, 1968), pp. 101, 202.

2. F. Elrington Ball, ed., *The Correspondence of Jonathan Swift, D.D.,* 6 vols. (London: Bell, 1910-14), 4: 167n.; Harold Williams, ed., *The Poems of Jonathan Swift,* 2d ed., 3 vols. (Oxford: Clarendon, 1958), 2: 491-92, hereafter referred to as *Poems;* Jonathan Swift, *Correspondence,* ed. Harold Williams, rev. David Woolley, 5 vols. (Oxford: Clarendon, 1963-72), 3: 410-11, 418, hereafter cited as *Corr.*

3. Henry Craik, *The Life of Jonathan Swift,* 2d ed., 2 vols. (1894; reprint ed. New York: Burt Franklin, 1969), 2: 184.

4. W. R. Scott, "James Arbuckle and His Relation to the Molesworth-Shaftesbury School," *Mind,* New Series 8 (1899): 194-215; see also Scott, *Francis Hutcheson* (Cambridge: University Press, 1900), pp. 32-36, 184.

5. Nearly all published accounts of Arbuckle contain gross errors; an exception is a paper by [T. P. C.] Kirkpatrick as summarized in "The Bibliographical Society of Ireland," *Irish Book Lover* 26 (May 1939): 103-4.

6. Attributions to Delany seem to start with "Particulars of the Life and Writings of Dr. Delany," *Gentleman's Magazine* 47 (1777): 315. For contemporary attributions see *A Funeral Apotheosis on the Tribunes* (Dublin, 1729/30; Foxon F286); a note in the *Old Dublin Intelligence,* 24 Jan. 1729/30; Martinus Gulliver, *The Censoriad* (London: Bickerton, 1730; Foxon B315), pp. 17, 22; and *The Lucubrations of Salmanazar Histrum, Esq.* (Dublin, 1730), quoted by Richard R. Madden, *The History of Irish Periodical Literature,* 2 vols. (1867; reprint ed. New York: Johnson Reprint, 1968), 2: 306.

7. I have used a microfilm, supplemented by a description kindly supplied by P. A. L. Jones, Keeper of Printed Books, National Library of Wales. To him I am grateful for the description, for information about the volume's provenance, and for permission to quote and reproduce portions of it here.

8. I have checked Foxon's first-line index; Margaret Crum, *First-Line Index of English Poetry, 1500-1800, in Manuscripts of the Bodleian Library, Oxford,* 2 vols. (New York: Modern Language Association, 1969); J. A. Leo Lemay, *A Calendar of American Poetry in the Colonial Magazines and in the Major English Magazines through 1765* (Worcester, Mass.: American Antiquarian Society, 1972); the Boys-Mizener first-line index to the miscellanies in Case's *Bibliography,* Spencer Research Library, University of Kansas; and the first-line indexes in the Huntington Library, the Osborn Collection at Yale University Library, and the Department of Manuscripts, British Library.

9. In the National Library of Ireland film of the Molesworth papers (n. 4081-82). I am indebted to the Director of the National Library of Ireland for permission to reproduce portions of this letter below. It has proved impossible to trace the original, sold at Sotheby's as a part of lot 106, 12 Dec. 1977. The letter is published in Historical Manuscripts Commission 55, *Various Collections,* VIII (1913), pp. 351-52.

10. Public Record Office of Northern Ireland, D531/2A/1-4/5, pp. 147-59. Public Record Office of Ireland, QRO Letter memorial, petition and report book, 1734-63, fols. 1 and 4, and from the other end of the volume, pp. [1-6]. Portions of both manuscripts are reproduced below by kind permission of the respective Deputy Keepers. It should be noted that the QRO letterbook is a volume of transcripts, and therefore one or two documents ostensibly co-signed by Arbuckle are not in his hand, having been copied into the book by another clerk. For further evidence of his employment in the Quit Rent Office, see *Pue's Occurrences,* 16-19 Jan. 1741/2.

11. The annotations, in a copy of the edition designated "R" in *Poems,* 2:491-99, agree with the Dublin printing (rpt. in *Poems*) except as follows: 55 With] In *NLW.* 57 *unannotated.* 126 Yet] Oh *NLW.* 172 Disclaim the] Disclaim both *NLW.* In *Poems* Williams fails to note that for "With" in line 133, R reads "By"; Arbuckle changes it to "With" in *NLW.*

12. Ornaments used by Faulkner (and presumably also James Hoey, his partner until about April 1730) appear in the following Dublin publications of 1730: by [Swift], *An Epistle upon an Epistle;* *A Libel on D— D—* (two editions); *To Doctor D—l—y, on the Libels Writ against Him;* *A Vindication of His Excellency the Lord C———t;* *Horace Book I, Ode XIV;* and *Traulus, the Second Part* [part I has no ornaments]. [Patrick Delany], *The Pheasant and the Lark, A Fable* (two editions); and James Blackwell, *A Friendly Apology for a Certain Justice of Peace.* I have compared these editions with the ornaments in Faulkner's edition of Matthew Pilkington's *Poems on Several Occasions* (1730), and have consulted the index of printers' ornaments in progress at the library of Trinity College, Dublin, under the direction of M. Pollard.

13. *Corr.,* 3: 410-11, 418; I am conflating remarks from the two letters.

14. I have examined and rejected as self-evidently implausible [William Dunkin], *A Vindication of the Libel* ([Dublin], 1729/30; Foxon D530); *Triplets on a Damn'd Letter of Abuse, to the Reverend Doctor D—la—y* (Dublin, 1729/30; copy in National Library of Ireland); James Blackwell, *A Friendly Apology* ([Dublin], 1730; Foxon S270); *An Epistle to a Certain Dean, Written Originally in Italian, by Carlo Monte Socio, Fellow of the Academy of the Humoristi in Rome, and Translated from the Vatican Manuscript. By a student in philosophy* (Dublin, 1730; Foxon E386); *The Paper Kite, a Fable* ([Dublin], 1729; Foxon P47).

15. Ball blandly calls it a "pretty reply" to Delany in *Swift's Verse: An Essay,* p. 251; Joseph Horrell examines its remarks on fable in his edition, *Collected Poems of Jonathan Swift* (London: Routledge and Kegan Paul, 1958), 2: 772-73, 792; and to the latter topic Richard H. Rodino returns in the present collection of essays. William Monck Mason has contended that it is "quite impossible" that Swift wrote the "Answer," referring to a footnote to *Some Seasonable Advice to Doctor D—n—y:* "Doctor,/There is an Answer to Your *Essay on Criticism* ready for the Press, and

likewise some Animadversions upon your Fable of the *Pheasant, &c.* by the same Hand, which has given you this Friendly Advice." However, it is not necessary to identify Swift's "Answer" with these "animadversions." (I have not found other animadversions upon Delany's fable, but neither have I identified the "Essay on Criticism" or the answer to it.) See Mason, *The History and Antiquities of the Collegiate and Cathedral Church of St. Patrick, near Dublin* (Dublin: printed for the author, 1819), p. 380n.

16. See *Poems,* 1:139-40n.; *Corr.,* 2:176.

17. The title-page ornament and the factotum in *An Answer* also appear in George Berkeley, *Alciphron* (Dublin: printed for Risk, Ewing, and Smith, 1732; printer unnamed): see the cancellans 2K8 (= 2R8) and leaf 2M1. In turn, two ornaments in *Alciphron,* leaves 2E4 and 2G2, occur respectively on the title page of [W. Maple], *A Method of Tanning without Bark* (Dublin: printed by A. Rhames, 1729), and in *A Tale of a Tub,* 7th ed. (Dublin: printed by A. Rhames for W. Smith, 1726), leaves C2 and M2. Certainly it has been impossible to link the ornaments in *An Answer* to George Faulkner's press.

18. For various kinds of assistance I am indebted to J. Baldwin, C. J. Benson, Andrew Carpenter, Mary Clapinson, A. C. Elias, Jr., Robert C. Elliott, Seamus Heaney, Daniel Huws, M. Pollard, G. J. Slater, David Woolley, and the staff of the University of Glasgow Archives.

Index